Tales from the Dáil Bar

Ted Nealon

Gill & Macmillan

Gill & Macmillan Ltd
Hume Avenue, Park West, Dublin 12
with associated companies throughout the world
www.gillmacmillan.ie

© Ted Nealon 2008
978 07171 4255 2

Typography design by Make Communication
Print origination by TypeIT Dublin
Printed by ColourBooks Ltd, Dublin

This book is typeset in 11.5 Minion on 14.5pt.

The paper used in this book comes from the wood pulp of
managed forests. For every tree felled, at least one tree is planted,
thereby renewing natural resources.

A CIP catalogue record for this book is available from the British
Library.

5 4 3 2

Contents

There is very little recognition of the extent to which being a public representative has ceased to be a one-person job. From councillor to minister, the elected representative needs the assistance and teamwork of the whole family, such are the demands and expectations on them.

I am fortunate in having this book to dedicate to my wonderful wife, Josephine, for all her sacrifices and sheer hard work, always with a smile! With all my love to her and our two children, Louise and Feargal.

Did you tell 'em the latest from the Dáil Bar?

For over thirty years, Leinster House, seat of the Dáil, was my 'local'.

During that long period, I was a journalist, a politician and I sometimes worked in political communications, a sort of hybrid of the two. I changed jobs many times but found that there was no advantage in changing pubs as well. So I stuck with Leinster House.

It has two bars. One is the Members' Bar, exclusively for the use of Dáil deputies and senators, and its forbidden territory gives it a certain air of mystique. You could meet anyone in the second, the public bar. On big days — the days of the set pieces — it is packed and noisy, a great place for drink, gossip and intrigue. At other times you might see a school group being looked after by the TDs from their constituency and perhaps the senators too: smiles all round, but somehow they don't look at ease.

There's little that's special about the Leinster House bars. Indeed they were probably more impressive in the time when it was the town house of the Fitzgeralds. Nothing there like the facilities enjoyed by MPs in the House of Commons, with over twenty bars around (one of them now referred to by the Irish as the 'Lord Fitt'). Dáil deputies used to be accused, especially by hecklers at election rallies, of getting drink at duty-free prices in Leinster House. 'Duty-free drink if you get elected, and it's free altogether if you head the poll,' used to be the taunt. I can verify that there never was anything in it, or, if there was, I was standing at the wrong counter for thirty years!

There are seldom any complaints with the Leinster House bars, and the service is excellent. The previous bar manager,

Seán Sheilds, retired recently after forty years of prompt and discreet service. If he had been a politician, he would have been father of the house. When it came to keeping order, I would say the bar manager, Seán, had a much easier time than the Ceann Comhairle in the chamber down the corridor. Throughout his time, the reputation for good stories, well told, continued to grow.

Dick Barry, a Fermoy deputy and minister, and a good man to tell a story himself, believes that the strong tradition of stories and anecdotes arose both out of the odd times of sittings (day and night) of the Dáil, and the lack of facilities for deputies around the house. 'They didn't have offices of their own. They had to write their letters by hand and even buy the stamps! Our offices were our pockets, and one Cork deputy had his tailor sew A4-size pockets to the inside of his macintosh. He used to say that he could stuff as much into them as a pair of creels.

'What else could we do in between the times we were required to vote, except to tell stories and anecdotes amongst ourselves in the bar, and one special thing we had going for us was that we'd never run out of material. If we were running low then there was plenty of talent around to compose new stories. I've been watching politicians come and go from Leinster House for a lifetime; the more I see, the more I'm convinced that there is a bit of a showman in every politician, certainly the ones that make it to the Dáil or Seanad. I remember in the 1950s, nearly every deputy was an aspiring raconteur, but it was hard going to get them to speak in the chamber.'

I have never heard a clear-cut definition of what qualifies a story for Dáil bar classification. If it's good enough it will get recognition. One sure sign that you're making progress is when you hear another TD — especially a colleague from your own constituency — telling one of your stories without making a fuss about the author.

The stories are best when they reflect what's happening down the corridor in the Dáil chamber, and typically consist of politicians poking fun at each other and their efforts in the national interest. Considering the confrontational nature of things in Leinster House, the political stories are 'moderate'. With a few discreet changes, much like the forming of governments in modern times, they can be transferred between the parties. However, when you see a group of politicians, exclusively from the one party, clustered closely together and laughing a little louder than usual, then you can be sure that the story being told is not for swapping. *Ach sin scéal eile!*

The times of Dáil sittings were greatly changed in the 1970s following a campaign mainly led by the Chief Whip of the Cosgrave/Corish government, John Kelly. He wanted more family-friendly working hours for politicians and, as he used to say himself, 'more experience for Irish parliamentarians of working in daylight!' Also, committees of the house have greatly extended their time and input into the legislative process; and politicians, at their own invitation, have expanded their investment in clinic work enormously until it has become something of a monster. All these changes have eaten into storytelling time, but the tradition still continues.

By acclaim if not by vote, the two star raconteurs — when they get the odd bit of free time — are the Tánaiste and Fianna Fáil deputy leader Brian Cowen, and Fine Gael leader Enda Kenny, whose father Henry was holder of the unofficial title in his day, along with his All-Ireland medal. Their stories come with parish perfect accents and the occasional song.

Most of the stories and anecdotes I have gathered here I took from political and journalist colleagues, and I thank them sincerely for them. One thing that we did notice, however, was that even some of the great James Dillon classics that first brought laughter at the fair of Carrickmacross, or when meeting the farmers as he crossed the drumlins on his way to Ballybay, were gradually slipping from memory, but not the Pig's toes.

Heckler: 'Mr Dillon, how many toes has a pig?'

Dillon: 'Take off your shoes and count!'

Acknowledgments

What do you do with acknowledgments for a book, which, apart from its compilation, is also virtually a trawl through your life? It must be said absolutely clearly that a collection like this is not possible without generous and enthusiastic help. This I got in massive measures through anecdotes, stories and encouragement. I wish to acknowledge the help of all.

Dick Barry, Myra Barry, Oliver Barry, Louis J. Belton, Andrew Boylan, Mike Burns, Don Conlon, Paul Conmy, Jimmy Deenihan, Bernie Doyle (no Bernie, no book), Seán Duignan, Dan Egan, Fergus Finlay, Seamus Finn, Des Fisher, Charles Flanagan, Jack Harte, Aidan Hennigan, Elinor Hickey, Phil Hogan, Joe Jennings, Mary Keane, Michael Kilcoyne, Brian Lenihan, Conor Lenihan, Joanne Loughnane, Benny McAree, Muiris MacConghail, Pádraic McCormack, Dinny McGinley, Paul McGrath, Maurice Manning, Enda Marren, Donald Menzies, Gina Menzies, Michael Mills, Gerry Murray, Louise Nealon, Mike Nealon, Mike Joe Nealon, David Norris, Conor O'Clery, Joan Raftery, Gerry Reynolds, Michael Ring, Chris Ryder, Kathleen Smith, John Stafford, Niall Stokes, Jonathan Williams.

Fergal Tobin, Liz Raleigh and Deirdre Rennison Kunz from Gill & Macmillan.

A special acknowledgment to Feargal Nealon, who, with a multitude of skills, helped bring the book to completion.

Seamus Loughnane, who loved these yarns, contributed many and insisted they become a collection.

1. The Vocation of Politics

Local Knowledge

I came from Coolrecull, Aclare, in County Sligo. Things were desperately tough when I was a growing lad in the 1930s. The farms had been divided down to what were unviable patches of land. Four to six cows was the general run before Europe came to the rescue. And if one or two of those cows turned out not to be in calf, in any one year it was a serious setback, and something of a disaster if it struck in successive years. The bull was usually blamed, though he was generally the innocent partner, according to later disease eradication research.

Families were large (five to ten children) and no jobs. 'We were rearing them for export' was how a local observer described things. 'The track of their schoolbags would not be off their backs before the American wakes were organised.' Then they were on their way to Queenstown or Galway to join the liners for New York, with 'the passage' paid by those already there. The eldest son might remain on to take over in due course, but very often he couldn't afford all those years of waiting around, so he took the boat and the youngest remained — often to end his days as a bachelor.

My father, also Ted, was the youngest in his family. He remained on while the others emigrated to America. He was in many ways a remarkable man. After leaving school at the age of fourteen, he went back there each year for the next four when the work on the land slackened around the end of October. The teacher, Pat Spellman, the principal of Kilmactigue Boys' School, took a special interest in this unusual pupil but there were no further volunteers.

Tragically my father's young wife Una, my mother, died when I was only two and my brother, Mike Joe, was four years old. Tuberculosis was then sweeping through the countryside. The only visual memory I have of my mother is the lid of the coffin leaning against the wall of the house as they prepared to take her to the church. Our father looked after my brother and myself in an extraordinary way. The only thing we were short of was money and at that time so was nearly everyone else.

My father had an astounding memory, a wonderful gift of retention. If you asked him what sort of day it was on Easter Saturday ten years previously, he would have a shot at it. Maybe someone local had got married on that day and he'd then recall the kind of weather they'd had for the wedding breakfast. A neighbour, Tom Bán, also had 'great recall', as they would describe it. He and my father sometimes set themselves memory challenges, if they met one another going out to the fields or to the bog. I'd be sent later to check out on how Bán was doing.

My father had a special interest in politics, although I must say that, in spite of knowing the politics of the whole parish down to the last few votes, he never, directly to me or I think to anyone else, revealed whom exactly he voted for himself. Political allegiances in the area were divided fairly evenly and because of family connections there was a general assumption on how his vote went. But I could never say with any degree of certainty whether that assumption was right or otherwise.

It was a Sunday in the summer of 1938. Dr Martin Brennan

was standing on a low dry-stone wall opposite the gates of Tourlestrane church, in the parish of Kilmactigue in south Sligo, waiting for the congregation to come out from Second Mass. He was our local doctor and since the previous week had become the local Dáil deputy (Fianna Fáil, Sligo–Leitrim). He was back at his own church to thank those attending Second Mass for their support in the general election (he had already been there after First Mass).

It wasn't a bragging or boastful performance. It was more a local man thanking his neighbours for the turn they had done him. And all stopped and listened out of respect, whatever they had done when they had the 'pencil with the power' in their hands.

What followed turned the whole occasion into a kind of magic for me ... all of eight years old. Reading from the back of an old twenty box of Goldflake cigarettes, the doctor told us the exact number of votes he had got in each of the polling stations in the whole parish — and there were a lot that time, including one in Slack's house in my own townland of Coolrecull. The only thing we had really been taught about elections at school, in those sensitive times, was that they were absolutely secret, that no one could ever know or find out how a person had voted. But with the figures now available, sure I could nearly do Coolrecull myself! My father, who had been at First Mass, wasn't there to explain it for me, so I asked a neighbour how it was done.

'Maybe they had a little man inside in the boxes counting,' he suggested to me, but he couldn't hold back his smile. 'Sure what does a little lad like you want to know about these grown-up things?'

Instead of the answer I wanted, he gave me a penny with the King George v head on it and told me to run down to Mary Meehan's for sweets before she closed the shop. He was a kindly man and always gave me something, but I suspected that on this occasion it could have been a tactical move — he didn't know the answer himself. The growing skills of the tallymen were coming as a bit of a surprise to everyone.

The majority of farmers in this area at the foothills of the Ox mountains, stretching to Lough Talt on one side and to Tubbercurry on the other, were still guided by the Church regulation of no heavy work on a Sunday. For my father on this particular Sunday, it didn't matter anyhow because he had organised four of his neighbours to call to the house and go through the election figures — to give faces to the figures, as he put it. In other words, what they were about to attempt was to work out how everyone in the parish had voted, and they made little of it! This was all about local knowledge and they had plenty of that.

Between them, or maybe individually, they knew every house in the parish, who lived in each house, who was home from America or from England and who was coming home or going away. They knew the families who were related (first cousins, first cousins once removed) by birth, or connected by marriage; all this was very important, considering that political loyalties were more often handed down than thought out. They knew all those newly qualified to vote at twenty-one. One thing my brother, Mike Joe, and myself (allowed to listen as long as we remained quiet) did notice was that one of our neighbour 'analysts' was a man who originally hailed from the other end of the parish. This would be giving the team greater width (as Sir Alex Ferguson might have put it if he had been around at the time).

They wanted to get the work done fast because there would be a few ramblers around keen to know what was going on. Their methods were not very scientific, all based on their own knowledge and in the final analysis on their own judgment. But, on the other hand, they would not have been over-impressed with the margins of error professional pollsters allow themselves today. They made a good start by concentrating on the local candidate, Dr Brennan. If the tally showed that he had got four or five votes more than expected, then they had all the knowledge to work out where those had come from. After completing five or six townlands without leaving many doubt-fuls behind, the Coolrecull men ran into their first real problem: a small polling station where one candidate got four votes less than the absolute minimum forecast.

Tom Bán, the oldest in the group, had been out in the fresh air for a while and was now coming back.

'Bán is whistling and that's a good sign,' one of the neighbours said.

'You got it, Tom?' another asked as Bán walked in.

'Hell, no. Hell, no.... But didn't we hear some talk a couple of weeks ago that some girls had got telegrams from the Cunard White Star Line that their liner would be leaving a few hours earlier than scheduled from Queenstown, and giving them a new time for embarkation. I'm thinking now that maybe they had to leave ahead of the election voting starting. They were four certain votes for that candidate, and he could have done with them.'

There were no mobile phones in Coolrecull at that time, so they had to wait until that night for confirmation when Tomeen, a neighbour of the girls, was cycling home with his girlfriend. The guess was right. Tom Bán and the story of how he had figured out the voters who had waved good-bye was the talk of the place. 'That man should have been a detective,' everyone said.

The early embarkation was not unusual at the time. Apart from that minor hiatus of emigration, there were no other surprises in voting that could not have been explained by changes on the ballot paper.

One recurring problem, however, that the Coolrecull men were coming up against arose from a number of recent marriages. They knew all the people involved and all the politics involved in the pre-nuptial situation, but there was no guarantee that that's the way things would continue. In the end, a few went down as 'not sure'. The 'analysts' didn't like doing that but it was the only fair way until the new people had settled in. It was a problem that would increase as men and women travelled a bit further to explore marriage possibilities outside of the matchmaker's list!

Nemesis

Among his many supporters in south Sligo, where I grew up in the 1930s and 1940s, Dev was God and the *Irish Press* was the Gospel. All you had to do to find a man's politics was to see which newspaper his lunch was wrapped in going to the turf bog. If it was the *Irish Press*, then he was a Dev man; if it was not, then he was an anti-Dev man. There were no political gradients in between.

Establishment of the *Irish Press* was one of de Valera's political master strokes, in a stroke-full political career. Not only did it get him the continuous guaranteed backing of what was to become a powerful newspaper publishing house, it was his very own newspaper under his total control, editorial and otherwise, with the right to pass on that control to a chosen successor. As a junior reporter in the *Irish Press* newsroom, I found out — much to my surprise — the extent to which this editorial control could be a hands-on control by the man himself.

———

It was in 1954 and the day of the funeral in Ennis of Bishop Fogarty of Killaloe. Éamon de Valera was attending officially as the leader of the Opposition, and not in his more accustomed role of those times, as Taoiseach. It was a change of seating which, I am told, the man they were burying would not have regretted. At the same time, there was a by-election campaign in progress across the Shannon in Limerick West, and Fianna Fáil's headquarters in Upper Mount Street, Dublin, as always, had organised a Dev election rally for that night in Rathkeale. After all, there was no rule saying that you cannot mourn a bishop in one county and do a bit of electioneering in the next. It was a case of maximising the use of the leader's time.

At this stage, Dev did not use scripts for speeches at election rallies, presumably because of his failing eyesight. What he did instead was give a 'dictate' in advance to reporters of what he intended saying, so that they could file their reports in time for the early editions. Because Dev was extremely sensitive about being quoted accurately and even more sensitive about not being misquoted, the *Irish Press* always sent along their senior reporter, Niall Carroll. (Niall was a brother of Paul Vincent Carroll, the Abbey playwright, and an Abbey playwright himself *(The Wanton Tide)*.) Dev liked and trusted Carroll, who was an excellent shorthand note-taker and so could be relied on to get every word Dev uttered. On this occasion I myself was sent along with Niall, just to do the usual piece on the blazing tar barrels, the guard of honour of veterans, the paraffin-soaked sods of turf, and the rousing reception. It was just a question of checking the files for the last Dev rally and getting in the local names, or so I thought.

Our arrangement was to meet up with Mr de Valera in Carmody's Hotel after the funeral; this was always his place to stay when in Ennis. We were shown to a room where he and his private secretary were resting after a very busy morning, including a clinic. It was the first time I had come into close proximity with this great man of Irish history. He was stretched out, hands under his head, on an old, brass-knobbed double bed. He gave us a courteous welcome, apologised for his clinic over-running ('they all wanted to see me personally') and, before starting his dictation, ensured that there would be a meal ready for us when we had finished our interview. A very charming man indeed. About twenty minutes into his dictation, and much to my surprise, Niall Carroll got up and said: 'Excuse me, Chief, but I have to get this off to the office because of the early editions. Mr Nealon will carry on from here.' It was an unexpected upgrading from the tar barrel piece for a rather dodgy shorthand note-taker!

Dev got quickly back to his dictation and to prices — the failure to bring them back to 1951 levels. For this he blamed John A. Costello, the Taoiseach, and his colleagues in government. It was obvious that this was not going to be a de Valera, the statesman, speech. This was a Dev who had some serious business to do in the next few days, like helping to win the Limerick West seat in the by-election for Fianna Fáil candidate Michael Colbert.

> Everyone listening to me knows that I am speaking the truth. The reports of the General Election speeches in the newspapers (of the parties now forming the Coalition Government), the leaflets distributed to your homes, the slogans in the large posters on the walls — slogans that still remain on some of these walls — all proclaim the truth of what I say.... The Coalition leaders promised that, if they were put in as a government in our stead, that bread would come down to 6d. a loaf, tea to 2/8 a lb., the pint would come back to 11d. and corresponding reductions would take place in cigarettes, tobaccos, beer and spirits. The prices of all these had been put up by Fianna Fáil because they wanted people to eat less, drink less and to be less comfortable.

He was warming to his subject and talking of a Coalition deception on how they would bring down prices. Then he came up with the phrase 'Nemesis is at the heels of the Coalition.' After dictating for a few further minutes he said: 'Mr Nealon, would you ever mind reading back that piece about Nemesis?'

With a bit of help from his private secretary, Pádhraig Ó hAnnracháin, who was taking his own notes, I did that.

'Now, Mr Nealon, you might tell the editor of the paper that that piece about Nemesis might make a good lead paragraph for the report of my speech,' he said and continued with his dictation for another few minutes. Again he asked for the Nemesis piece to be read out.

'Mr Nealon, you might tell the editor that that might make a good front-page headline for my speech,' he said.

After finishing phoning in my section of the dictation, I gave the editor the instructions I had got from the Chief (everyone around was using the title. No problems there). Lieutenant-Colonel Mattie Feehan, the editor of *The Sunday Press*, was a man who, if asked, would die for de Valera, never mind give him the banner headline he wanted.

When Niall Carroll and I got to Rathkeale, the rally was over and the pubs were packed. We met Pádhraig Ó hAnnracháin on our way to the pub where the Fianna Fáil hierarchy were relaxing.

'You won't believe me,' he told us, 'but the Chief forgot about Nemesis entirely. Never a mention of Nemesis.'

We all had a laugh at the expense of the Chief, but we did not regard it as any great crisis. We had the report of the speech sent in and it would appear exactly as per instructions, but the private secretary knew his man. And he knew that the following morning when the papers were being read to him, Dev would realise that he had forgotten about Nemesis. That's not the kind of thing he would easily dismiss. With the remaining diehards from the crowd still cheering, and before Dev could get off the platform, the private secretary whispered the one word 'Nemesis' in his ear. Back went Mr de Valera to the microphone. Out they came or out they were pushed from the pubs. And for the best part of ten minutes the Chief, with as much care and precision as if he were explaining the oath, told them about

Nemesis and the speech they would be reading in the papers the following morning.

'I think it would be very unfair on you, good people of Rathkeale and west Limerick who turned up here, to read in the papers something that I was supposed to have said but actually did not say. So I am saying it to you now,' he finally wound up. 'Nemesis is at the heels of the Coalition.'

Sadly, it was anything but a typical end to one of Dev's rallies, still remembered for their organisation, enthusiasm and excitement. It was as flat as the pints waiting for their owners in the pubs in Rathkeale. But they cheered him again anyway and the following Wednesday were out in force to give him victory in the Limerick West by-election.

Canvassing around the Parlour

Very few candidates honestly like elections. The hazard of losing your seat is always there, whether you're a poll topper or a poll squatter. If it can happen in politics, it does.

One man, Joe Sheridan, independent Dáil deputy for Longford–Westmeath for sixteen years from 1961 (in 1965 he was one of only two independents elected to the Dáil), relished one aspect of all general elections: the 'canvassing of the convents'. This was a time-honoured ritual. All candidates and all parties were welcome to come along — but by appointment only. This was presumably in the interests of good order, or it may have been a solution imposed by a Rome-trained bishop to prevent any embarrassing inter-party conflict from breaking out on holy ground.

It led to a pile of anecdotes and stories haycock high, and this one is told by Louis J. Belton, former deputy and senator in the same area. For the canvass, Joe Sheridan always had his great friend and election agent Harry Skelly. He sometimes referred to Harry as his *Chef de Cabinet*. They were both equally good and between them left very few stray votes behind. There was no need for rehearsals, they knew each other so well: just a reminder from Joe to Harry not to forget to mention the monsignors. This was a reference to two brothers of Joe's who were making a considerable impact in their work on the American mission. Both were great men in the pulpit.

The Sheridan canvassers were welcomed by the Reverend Mother in the parlour and at the first lull of the conversation, Harry asked Joe how the monsignors were.

'Fine,' said Joe, and went on to talk at length, which was very unusual for Joe, although a fine speaker. He impressed the nuns with his knowledge of Church affairs, and you could see from Harry's face that he was very pleased with how his man was doing.

Then Joe went on to talk about his sister, Sister Gertrude, and how things weren't near as good with her. The Reverend Mother asked what the difficulty was.

'She's in South America, where the regime is much less friendly than it was and is making things difficult for the teaching orders in particular.' All the sisters would pray for her that night.

On the way out to the car, Joe and Harry compared notes and both thought they had done very well. There had been a good turnout and Joe had a few friends, in-house nuns who supported his politics and would look after his interests on election day. As Joe was about to start the car, Harry leaned over.

'Well, Joe, in all the time I've been with you down the years, and all the campaigns we've fought together, would you believe that is the first time that I ever knew you had a sister a nun.'

'Nor do I, Harry,' said Joe, 'Nor do I, Harry — I just threw her in for luck!'

2. One-Liners

A Perfect Solution

At a meeting of the Borough Council of a southern town, it seemed that no one was too happy with the traffic flow at a new car park. Even the engineering staff accepted that there were some changes needed in the lay-out. They needn't have worried. Help was at hand. A Councillor, well known for his inventive mind, was about to give them the solution.

'I have it,' he said. 'What we need are two exits. An exit in and an exit out!'

Save the World

All the Sunday papers were predicting a 'tricky' meeting of the Labour Party, with a rough ride forecast for the leadership. The back-up stories seemed to be based entirely on 'leaks', but at the time that was a fairly normal means of internal communication. On this occasion it seems that at least two sources were doing the spinning. It was the kind of speculation the leadership could not ignore.

The leader of the Labour Party at the time was Frank Cluskey and the chairman of the Labour Parliamentary Party was Michael D. Higgins. Working together, they were a formidable combination.

In the end there was a clash of dates for Michael D. He was away in South America attending an important meeting of the World Peace Organisation. He couldn't make it back in time for the Labour Party's tricky meeting.

When word got to Frank Cluskey that he would be without his chairman, his comment was: 'That's typical of Michael D. Give him the choice of saving the world or of saving the Labour Party, and he'll always go for the easy option.'

Oliver's Car

Oliver J. Flanagan first stood as a candidate for the Monetary Reform Party in Laois–Offaly and was elected. As everyone knows, in that campaign he got around by bicycle. In the meantime he bought a new car and was able to get to meetings everywhere in the five-seat constituency. At one of these meetings, while he was addressing the crowd, this fellow kept interrupting, shouting: 'What about Monetary Reform? Tell us about Monetary Reform.'

In the end Oliver said: 'I'll tell you about Monetary Reform. I came to this town at the last election on a bicycle. Now look over there. Do you see that car? That's my car, and that's what I'm driving today. Now,' he said, 'that's Monetary Reform.'

Ned O'Keeffe

Ned O'Keeffe (Fianna Fáil, Cork East) has been a popular member of Dáil Éireann since winning his seat in the second general election of 1982. In 1997 Bertie Ahern appointed him Minister of State at the Department of Agriculture and Food, with special responsibility for food. Ned ceased to hold office in 2001 amid some confusion in all parties as to whether he had formally resigned or had been asked to do so by the Taoiseach.

It seems to me that very few deputies know with absolute certainty the precise situation.

I was asked for my opinion at the time by a number of colleagues I met socially at a race meeting, in Sligo, I think. I offered them this piece of advice, while acknowledging that it fell short of the enlightenment they sought: 'There are now two great mysteries in Irish politics — who shot Michael Collins, and who shot Ned O'Keeffe!'

The Last Man Out Wash the Glasses

After many years in journalism and in politics, I must have acquired some expertise or wisdom in predicting how newcomers to the top in politics will fare. Will they bend under the new pressures around them or will they stick the heat? Experience does help.

One person whose reaction I could never figure out with any great confidence was that of former Taoiseach Liam Cosgrave. He seemed to meet with equanimity whatever came along, both good news and bad. For three years I worked directly to him as head of Government Information Services or press secretary to the Taoiseach. Throughout that time I found it very hard to detect any change in his demeanour, whatever the pressures. He was never bothered with camera angles. I once said that he was happiest the day he got no publicity at all!

It surprised most people to learn that he was a witty, humorous man, who told stories as good as any that came from the Dáil bar. When he travelled outside Dublin I was often in the accompanying group. On one particular day we were heading westward. He had an important job to do, and arrangements were made for a break. The proprietor of the pub where we stopped was an affable but ageing man who had a great welcome for the Taoiseach. However, there was a problem: the pub itself could compete in any league for the title of dirtiest pub in Ireland. What fascinated me were the walls. Tweed suits and shawls had rubbed against them for decades, and they looked for all the world like cow houses before EC milk parlours took their place: black, shiny and rounded from the passing cows and in need of a lick of paint. Not that anyone seemed to mind.

Later, leaving the pub, I was with the Taoiseach's security man, just ahead of Liam Cosgrave. The Taoiseach was a very brisk walker and soon caught up with us, stopped us, looked at the detective sergeant, looked at me and pointed to the pub:

'I hear they did it up recently!' said he.

John Kelly

At a meeting of the Fine Gael Parliamentary Party, John Kelly (Dublin South-East) told his colleagues that he feared they were of the opinion that speeches somehow wafted to him through the air when he was having a bath, and all he had to do was keep the notepaper dry!

He was once again being nominated as the party's final speaker in a major debate in progress in the Dáil chamber. He was very conscious of the honour but also of the work involved (he did his own typing on an old Olivetti machine). When speaking from the Opposition benches, he could lift the mood and morale of his party, invariably leaving behind some memorable quotes, as in Ballyhaunis in 1981 — 'the state is like a sow being rent by a farrow of cannibal piglets.'

John Kelly is one of the forgotten people of politics of recent times. He was Minister for Industry and Commerce, Minister for Foreign Affairs, Attorney General, Government Chief Whip and Chief Whip of Fine Gael. Parallel with his career in politics, he was Professor of Jurisprudence and Roman Law at UCD, and the author of *The Irish Constitution*. He was also a novelist!

Although John Kelly appeared to many as too free a spirit for the role of Chief Whip, his popularity with the deputies meant that he had no difficulty in lining up his members when the division bells called and he had considerable success in heading off some of the potential conflicts within the party. What he could not easily tolerate, however, was the raising again of issues he felt had been disposed of. 'The trouble with us in Fine Gael', he once said at a meeting of the Parliamentary Party, 'is that we can never pass a sleeping dog without having to go over and kick it.'

Junkets

Junkets we shall always have with us. Despite regular maulings from the media and follow-up taunts from constituents, nothing is going to stop the trail of political delegations going to see how their counterparts are doing in other parts of the country and elsewhere, especially elsewhere. Some of these cannot be defended. They are junkets in reality and, even more so, in the mind-sets of the participants, but it is only right to say that some of them can be extremely valuable. A very good example of this would be the British-Irish Parliamentary Association. Anyone who knows of the workings and meetings of that group will realise how valuable a role it played during the most delicate times of the Northern Ireland peace process.

Generally the Irish appear to relax a bit more on junkets abroad than when they are around Leinster House or in their constituencies. Maybe it's the brief respite from the burden of constituency work.

Among the trips still occasionally recalled is a group from the Houses of the Oireachtas to Vienna in the 1950s, although no one seems too clear what the purpose of the delegation was or who were the delegates, except for James Collins of Fianna Fáil and Teddy Lynch of Fine Gael. Both senior deputies, James Collins represented Limerick West from 1948 to 1968, and Teddy Lynch represented Waterford, holding the old Redmond seat and the Ballybricken vote. The two men were good friends and both loved the game of hurling. Teddy was a great man for music and a founder member of the Waterford International Festival of Light Opera. James Collins, like many another Limerick man, would probably have preferred a night at the dogs to a night at the opera, but the highlight of their entertainment programme was arranged for the famous Vienna Opera House.

Despite the surroundings, some of the Irish delegation were tired after the travel and meetings during the day and one or two of them nodded off. Not Teddy. He loved it all and had brought opera glasses with him. He led the applause. When that grew into a standing ovation, he was one of the first on his feet. It took James Collins and some others a little time to adjust to their surroundings with all the cheering.

'Where are we, Teddy?' James asked. 'What's all the cheering about?'

'Mooncoin', said Teddy, 'have scored another point.'

Albert's Iceberg

A few days after Albert Reynolds resigned as Taoiseach in December 1994, his press secretary, Seán Duignan, was interviewed on RTÉ by Gerry Ryan, who marvelled that a Taoiseach with so much going for him — peace in Northern Ireland, a vibrant economy, the largest majority in the history of the state — could have let his government go down the plughole so rapidly. How did Duignan feel watching it happen?

Duignan replied: 'I felt like the parrot on the great ocean liner watching the ship's magician perform his big disappearing trick. Just as he cried "Abracadabra", the liner struck an iceberg, and almost instantly went down by the bow, leaving nothing but a few bits of flotsam, onto which the parrot fluttered, looked around and said: "Fantastic. How the **** did he do that?"'

Albert sent word to Diggie that he was not amused.

The *Claudia*

Two weeks after the National Coalition government of Fine Gael and Labour took office, with Liam Cosgrave as Taoiseach, the new Minister for Defence, Patrick S. Donegan, gave the clearance that enabled a naval party to board a ship off the Waterford coast. The ship was the *Claudia*, Cyprus-registered, but this trip originated in Libya and, as it subsequently emerged, had been under surveillance throughout the journey.

On board was Joe Cahill, a leading IRA figure. He was later to face a court and was sentenced to three years' imprisonment. It was stated in court that the *Claudia*'s cargo hold and lifeboats had 250 rifles, 240 bayonets, 850 rifle magazines, 243 pistols, more than 20,000 rounds of ammunition, 10 anti-tank mines, 500 high-explosive grenades, gelignite and TNT explosives.

The *Claudia* was arrested off Helvick Harbour, County Waterford and brought to Cobh where it was searched and unloaded. Then, after the now famous 'kick up the transom', it was released.

The RTÉ security correspondent, Tom McCaughren, was the man interviewing the Minister, who was obviously thoroughly briefed by his Department on what to say and what not to say. When all the essential questions had been asked and answered, Tom tried one of those deliberately vague queries often thrown out on such occasions in the hope of tempting the Minister perhaps a little bit further than he had planned.

'Was there anything Minister Donegan would like to say about the intended purpose of the huge quantities of lethal weapons found aboard?'

From Minister Donegan came this response: 'It's not for me to speculate on the intended purpose. But it wasn't to shoot ducks!'

3. My Esteemed Colleagues

Willie O'Brien and the Dog

More than anyone else in Dáil Éireann, Willie O'Brien was a man who loved practical jokes, even when he was on the receiving end himself, as his colleagues ensured that he frequently was. The quality of the prank was everything as far as Willie (Fine Gael, Limerick West) was concerned, not the embarrassment of the victims.

As chairman of his parliamentary party and with his easy manner, he was often able to resolve disputes and settle 'turf wars' between supposed colleagues. This semi-official role never curtailed his activities to generate a bit of fun. Sometimes his plots were outrageous and could be carried off only by Willie himself. Occasionally someone might express some doubt — not criticism, of course — about Willie's 'pranks'. Were they really appropriate for a chairman of a major political party? These soundings never got anywhere and his colleagues ensured that he didn't run out of ideas.

Deputy O'Brien's own favourite prank, he told me, was one now generally referred to as 'The Dog at the Ard-Fheis'. It was the weekend of the Fine Gael Ard-Fheis meeting, usually held in Dublin at that time. After the week's work in the Dáil and the

Senate, the Oireachtas members were not on the trail to their constituencies but were awaiting the arrival of their delegates to join them in Dublin. The extra few hours at their desks gave them an opportunity to clean up some awkward problems with which they'd struggled for maybe months.

After completing their constituency work, quite a few of them gathered in the very large Fine Gael party rooms for a rest and a chat. (These rooms were the only accommodation that party members had available to themselves exclusively at that time.) Willie was there. So was Eugene Gilhawley (Sligo–Leitrim, my predecessor), Dinny McGinley (Donegal), a group of about seven in all.

In the distance at the other end of the large room was another Fine Gael colleague. We'll call him Pat Murphy (not his real name). It was Eugene Gilhawley who first spotted the potential of the situation.

'Maybe Deputy Murphy might like to join us. There's a phone extension down there where he's resting.' It was obvious that Deputy Murphy was a bit tired after the long day spent preparing for his delegates' arrival. Willie O'Brien needed no more encouragement except what he gave to himself. 'Willie boy, you're a winner!'

He first went to the bottom end of the Fine Gael rooms and with the help of his friends on the Leinster House switchboard (Willie had friends everywhere) he got through to the absolutely right extension. It didn't even require Deputy Murphy to turn around. Willie, at the extension farthest away, would be using the name Jack in his passable Dublin accent. Murphy picked up the receiver:

'Who are you looking for?' he asked finally when he got to say something.

'Is that Deputy Murphy? I come from your constituency, but I'm now living in Dublin. The word at home is that you're doing a great job. That you're a very hard-working TD and a smart man as a bonus,' came the voice of Jack (Willie).

'Well now, that might be a bit over the top.... People are very kind. I do my best.'

'Your almighty best as I'm told. In my part of North Dublin there used to be a Dáil deputy called Seán Dunne with his own poster: "If Dunne can't do it, it can't be done." ... I'm told that's you down to the last letter. You should do a bit more self-promotion. It never pays to be a modest politician.'

'Are there any members of your family still in my constituency? Would I know any of them?' asked Deputy Murphy.

'To tell you the truth, there's the best part of a quota, Deputy. I have three brothers and three sisters, all married, all with families. I'm nearly broke buying them presents. For some reason they all want dogs. It would be cheaper for me to set up a kennel.'

'Now if there is anything that I can do for you at any time, I'll be only too pleased to help. And, of course, the same goes for the family down in the constituency,' said Deputy Murphy.

'Sure I know that.... Now as you mentioned it, there's a little job that you might be able to do for me tomorrow. I have a dog — I call them all Lassie — to send down to my sister. It's very difficult to get a dog, even a red setter, on the bus, but no problem at all to pop them in the boot.... Where can I meet you?'

'Unfortunately — and I say so with great regret — I can't help you on this occasion. This is the weekend of the Fine Gael Ard-Fheis and I'm not travelling down to the constituency. I have to attend a lot of meetings here in Ballsbridge. They seem to like me as a chairman.'

'Well the time aspect is not that important', said Jack (Willie). 'It would do if you brought Lassie down next weekend.... Is there any place there at Leinster House that you could keep her in the meantime? I'm sure the FitzGeralds had kennels when they were there (Garret might know) and didn't the RDS run a Dog Show there?'

'You couldn't possibly bring a dog into Leinster House, for security reasons,' said Deputy Murphy in his best committee chairman style.

'I thought Lassie might add to the security,' said Jack, 'and she doesn't bite.'

At this stage Deputy Murphy felt that maybe some of the prank specialists among his colleagues were at work. He turned round to survey the room and he was thinking of one man in particular. Frantic signals went out to Willie to move himself fast.

'I saw the signals,' he told me afterwards. 'But I felt it all needed a bit of rounding off. And do you know what I started doing — barking into the phone! I think the laughing put the good Deputy off the trail. It was still a bit too close!'

Cool Fionn

The newly elected Dáil deputy had a few representations to make to the Department of Local Government arising from his clinic work. Actually the man he had first thought of contacting was the Minister in charge in that department or his Parliamentary Secretary. He was advised by the Department that that approach would only delay things because hundreds of representations arrived daily. There was a special division to deal with the issues raised by Dáil deputies. And the man to get on to was Fionn McCool.

Some confusion arose along the line, and after introducing himself, the new Deputy asked for Brian Boru.

'You're looking for the wrong man, Deputy. There's no Brian Boru here, but there is a Fionn McCool, and that's me. What's your problem?'

Cormac Breslin

When the Dáil becomes rowdy, the objective of the Ceann Comhairle (Chairman of the House) is to get things back in order as quickly as possible with a minimum of fuss, without having to ask any member to leave the Chamber and without having to adjourn the Dáil for a cooling-off period. Cormac

Breslin, Ceann Comhairle for the years 1967 to 1973, was very good at this kind of thing and much respected by all sides of the house.

At times Cormac tended to make the occasional comment, to himself really, in a sort of penetrating whisper that could be clearly heard by the reporters in the Press Gallery immediately behind his elevated chair. His greatest problems, often leading to 'uproar in the House', generally originated from Gerry l'Estrange (Fine Gael, Longford–Westmeath), then very active as Chief Whip of his party. On this particular day, even with Deputy l'Estrange not present, the Dáil was rowdy enough. So when Cormac saw Gerry speeding through the lobby like one of his own greyhounds breaking in Shelbourne Park, he knew things were not going to improve for the Chair and he may just have allowed his feelings to dominate for a moment. In his whisper he was overheard saying something like: 'Things were bad enough without that f—— l'Estrange getting involved.' Then he proceeded with the work of the House, and called on the next speaker: 'Deputy l'Estrange'.

Ombudsman

When Michael Mills was appointed by the Garret FitzGerald government as the country's first national Ombudsman in 1984, there was a general welcome for him, across the political divides, although it has to be said that Charles J. Haughey was not an admirer.

Before his appointment, Mills was for twenty years the political correspondent of the *Irish Press* and a regular panellist on the RTÉ political programme *The Hurler on the Ditch*. To be the chief political writer on a paper founded to promote and nourish Fianna Fáil and still maintain his independence was a difficult and delicate job, which Mills did admirably. He was regarded by most readers and viewers as 'a fair-minded man who talked a lot of sense'. It was a valuable reputation for him to have, moving to his new job of Ombudsman. This, in essence, was the investigation of complaints by citizens at the way they had been treated, but confined to, at first, a limited number of departments of State. Through the good work of Michael Mills in laying the foundations, the remit of the Ombudsman's office was greatly extended down through the years.

The Ombudsman was a new force at work for the rights of citizens, not always welcomed by some senior civil and public servants, who already had to deal with the complaints of politicians collected on their clinic trails. Michael Mills likes to tell a story of a case where all these forces came into play.

The complaint came to him originally by way of a letter from a lady who had been turned down by the Department of Social Welfare following her application for a Deserted Wife's Benefit after her husband had gone off to England. Mills and his office investigated it and their conclusion was that the complainant was right about her entitlement and that the Department should reverse its decision. From the start, it was always going to be a difficult case since it involved the filling in of a form with the potentially confusing question: 'Did your husband leave of his own volition?' The first reaction of the complainant was to seek the assistance of her local Dáil deputy in the filling in of the form.

Naturally Mills never divulges the name of the complainant and also never gives any kind of clue whatsoever as to the identity of the Dáil deputy. He simply calls him 'Murphy'. Deputy Murphy, from what one can gather, will never figure in the records as a great constituency worker. In turn though, it has to be said, there was no better deputy in Leinster House to make political capital out of what work he did do and sometimes out of the work done by one or other or both of his constituency colleagues. This is always a danger in a multi-seat constituency. If Murphy was in the mining business, he would be known as a man with potential as a 'claim jumper'.

When he was asked for advice in the deserted wife's case, he felt that the correct answer to the 'own volition' question was 'no'. It took the office of the Ombudsman, with the personal intervention of Michael Mills himself on several occasions, about five years to sort that out. The detailed arguments are given in Michael Mills's memoir, *Hurler on the Ditch*, an important book considering the special sources of information available to Michael as a political writer in the 1960s and 1970s, and as a man trusted and respected by Taoiseach Seán Lemass.

Throughout the long negotiations, members of the Ombudsman's office, and indeed Mills himself, had got to know the complainant: 'We had a lot of sympathy for her because of what we considered a denial of her rights and we had the greatest admiration for her tenacity,' he says. 'Without a doubt she was extremely grateful for the way we stayed with her case when she was not very hopeful of success herself.

'Finally there was a breakthrough and the argument of the Ombudsman and his office was accepted. The result, factoring in back money and allowing for inflation, meant about £30,000 to the complainant.' After getting out to the complainant an official letter of notification of the decision, the Ombudsman and a few of his staff, in a most unusual move at this level, went the short distance to Doheny & Nesbitt's pub for a celebration. 'I felt that the woman herself would be pleased at being finally vindicated despite all the setbacks, and that in due course she would be in contact with us to tell us so,' said Michael. But there was never a message, never a word of any sort. Silence.

'I couldn't understand it and I suspected that the hand of Deputy Murphy was there at work somewhere. It was. Through his excellent contacts he knew that a decision was about to be made after all these years and that it would favour the complainant. He took the details quickly and sent off a letter with the news. Not only that. He drove out to her house to explain — or so it seemed — how he personally got the

Department to see that she was right all the time. The visit to her was the least he could do after the way she had been denied justice down the years. He mentioned in passing that he expected she would be getting a routine official letter of confirmation of the decision from the Ombudsman's office in a few days' time. She told Murphy she was delighted at the result but at the same time said that she was a little bit disappointed that Michael Mills, after all his attention, didn't get the job done himself. Deputy Murphy nodded as if in agreement, but told her that it wouldn't be right to say that Michael Mills did them any harm.'

Some months before his retirement, Michael Mills learned from a friend that the deserted wife had died.

'She's in heaven now, so she knows who got her case sorted out for her,' was Michael's response.

'I wouldn't be too sure of that,' said his friend. 'As you are aware, Deputy Murphy died a few years ago and, presumably, has also gone to heaven. With his reputation for "claim jumping", you'd never know who the man might have been talking to.'

Gentlemen

It could be argued that the new Dáil deputy, who still hadn't fully informed himself about the whereabouts of the facilities at Leinster House, was in bad luck that the only other man around at his time of need was Deputy James Dillon. Granted Deputy Dillon, who had first arrived in Leinster House as Dáil deputy for Donegal in 1932 before moving to the Monaghan constituency in 1937, had an unrivalled knowledge of the House, both as regards the buildings and how business was conducted there. He was also a most courteous man.

But he was punctilious in seeing the proprieties observed. Not the kind of man to shout at on the corridors of the House of the National Parliament: 'Can you tell me where the jacks are?'

Deputy Dillon was glad to provide all the information requested.

'You go down that corridor there,' he explained. 'Then you turn to the right. You'll find the door you are seeking straight ahead of you. Written on the door is the one word GENTLEMEN. Don't let that deter you.'

Jack faces up to it
— Michael Mills

In October 1970 Jack Lynch was attending the fifty-second anniversary of the foundation of the United Nations in New York when news was received of the acquittal of Charles J. Haughey and his co-accused, by a Dublin jury, of attempting to import illegal arms into Ireland.

Lynch called a press conference at the Irish Consulate just across the road from the UN, which was attended by myself, Raymond Smith of the *Irish Independent*, Tony Ring of *The Cork Examiner* and a couple of other journalists. Smith took over the conference, asking question after question of the Taoiseach until Lynch became exasperated and suggested to him there were other people at the conference who wanted to ask questions too. He turned to me and said: 'Michael, you wanted to ask a question.'

I recalled to him that Haughey, after leaving the Courtroom, had called on those who had initiated the prosecution to do the honourable thing — which was generally regarded as a call on the Taoiseach to resign. Did he regard this statement as a challenge to his leadership?

'If it is a challenge,' he said, 'I will meet it head-on.'

I had my story and shortly afterwards left the

conference to rush back to the telex room in the UN where I had arranged with one of the operators to stand by to send over my story to Dublin. I was just completing the transmission when I heard Ring and Smith arriving into the adjoining room. They sounded unhappy. The reason became clear when it emerged that Smith was annoying Ring by constant requests to check on something the Taoiseach had said at the conference. The climax was reached when Smith asked for about the fifth time for confirmation of something he claimed the Taoiseach had said.

'I can't find that in my notes,' Ring said impatiently. 'Where did you get that?'

'I read it in his face,' Smith replied.

Ring exploded. 'If you could read your f—— notes half as well as you could read his face, we might get some work done around here.'

The headline in the *Irish Press* the following day read: 'Lynch to Meet Haughey Challenge Head-On'. Jack Lynch arrived back in Dublin to be met by a phalanx of supporters. Charles Haughey was isolated and sent to the back benches for five years until Taoiseach Jack Lynch restored him to the front bench in 1975.

[Michael Mills: journalist, political correspondent of the *Irish Press*, writer, broadcaster and Ireland's first Ombudsman]

4. Memorable Lines

DAVID NORRIS [from the Seanad]

Emancipated Literacy!
On the order of business one day my colleague and neighbour waxed lyrical on the subject of literacy. However, he got his terms a little mixed up and bewailed what he described as 'the high levels of adult literacy in Ireland', repeating the phrase several times. It was perfectly obvious that he meant illiteracy, but I couldn't resist the opening. I stood up and said:

'I completely agree with my colleague, Senator Costello, and share his horror at the high levels of adult literacy in Ireland. Already as we speak, the uneducated in this country are beginning to read and if something is not done soon, they will be writing as well. This is where Catholic Emancipation leads!'

No Offence Taken
In the early days, the fact that I was gay caused consternation among many of my colleagues. One of them described me as a 'pervert' once when I had just left the chamber. The next day he

was forced by the House to withdraw the comment and apologise for the insult. I felt compassion for the poor fellow as well as a desire to wind him up a bit, so I said in reply:

'The apology was quite unnecessary as I have not in fact been insulted. One can only be insulted by people one respects and he knows perfectly well that I have no respect for him whatever.'

We subsequently became good friends!

The Sinking Ship

When my colleague and pal Shane Ross joined Fine Gael a number of years ago, I couldn't believe it at first, but when it was confirmed I did refer to it on the order of business in the Senate. I said:

'Shane has shown characteristic courage but an uncharacteristic lack of *nous* or political astuteness, as most rats jumped *off* sinking ships whereas, on this occasion, Shane was actually jumping *on* to one.'

From Hill 16

For the big jobs, from Versailles to the Áras, Dev liked to pick the small man Seán T. Ó Ceallaigh. This led to a problem on All-Ireland final day.

'Would someone cut the grass. I want to see the president,' said the voice from the Hill.

[David Norris]

James Dillon

'When I first came to Monaghan to seek a Dáil seat in the general election of 1937, they said I hadn't the chance of a snowball in hell. Well now, after all these years, I'm the only snowball left.'

James Dillon was in full flight speaking in the Diamond in Monaghan town. The huge crowd, stretching from the Courthouse steps to well down the Dublin Road, was loving it. To add a bit to the tension — always there in Monaghan politics anyway — the whisper swept around that Dr Conor P. Ward, Parliamentary Secretary in a de Valera government, and a 'melted snowball' in Dillon's metaphor, had been embedded in a friend's house on the Diamond. He was no longer part of the action, but still keen to be near. It was the final Fine Gael rally of the 1954 general election — the perfect setting for James Dillon the orator.

It was my first time to hear him in action on a platform. Later I listened to him on many occasions, in the Dáil, at Fine Gael Ard-Fheiseanna in the Mansion House, Dublin, at church gates and at many a fair around the country. How good was he?

He was great when the crowd was friendly and he was even better when the crowd was hostile. The heckler was his best friend. Maurice Manning, in his excellent book *James Dillon, a Biography*, described him as probably the best Irish orator of the twentieth century. A big claim, but I'm certain that the vast majority of politicians who heard him from the platform would go along with that judgment.

Looking down from the vantage-point of the Press Gallery in Leinster House on some of the great set occasions, with Éamon de Valera as Taoiseach on the government side and right across the floor James Dillon in eloquent flow on behalf of the opposition, many of the journalists felt that, despite the hard words spoken that day and many other days, Dev admired, maybe even enjoyed, Dillon's performances.

Dillon, in his turn, recognised de Valera's supreme talent for obfuscation. In the Dáil he would describe his frustration at being unable to establish where exactly Dev stood, what exactly he had meant by what he had said.

'When you think you have him finally nailed down on what he did say or did not say, he will tell you to move that comma here over there, and that full stop over there back here, and what he said or is supposed to have said will mean something different entirely. And, dammit, it will. Such is the genius of the man.'

Many of Dillon's good speeches, and certainly the most entertaining ones, were given at party meetings behind closed doors (or half-closed doors might be more accurate in the case of Fine Gael meetings), so no record of these remains. As far as television is concerned, the coverage of politics was developing only when he retired, so the range of footage available is relatively limited and indicates what a performer he would have been on the modern screens.

His last speech to a Fine Gael gathering was given at a function in the Mansion House, Dublin, in 1983 to celebrate the sixtieth anniversary of Cumann na nGael and the fiftieth anniversary of Fine Gael. I had the honour of presiding at that gathering. James Dillon had retired by then and was adamant that he would no longer be available to speak on such occasions. However, in the Mansion House, he finally had to yield to the demands from the floor. His speech was a short one by his standards but Dillonesque to the end. Although Garret FitzGerald's government was in power at the time, Fine Gael, not unusually it has to be said, was divided on some issue. He could have ignored this entirely but after fifty-five years of speaking his mind from the time he started in Donegal, he wasn't going to change now. He gave his views on the issue. He spoke of the need for discipline and support for the leadership. Anyone who couldn't stick the heat should leave the kitchen.

Whatever his profile nationally, whatever work he had to undertake for his party as leader and otherwise, James Dillon always remained a very practical politician in minding his constituency as if he was a backbencher in a long-count marginal. Indeed, he occasionally boasted in the Dáil that in all his time as TD for Donegal from 1932 to 1937 and subsequently for Monaghan, there was never a constituency letter to which he did not reply. Not much of a boast nowadays where deputies, quite rightly, have offices, secretaries and the latest communications technology. Indeed, some deputies seem to have mastered the art of getting replies out before the actual requests come in. In Dillon's days what TDs had by way of office was what they carried around with them. Martin Corry, a veteran Cork deputy (and no friend of Dillon), always had his tailor sew letter-friendly pockets into his jackets and mackintoshes. 'They'd hold as much as a pair of creels,' he used to say.

Much of Dillon's correspondence, especially in later years, had to do with agricultural matters. Amongst them was a letter in 1951 from a Colonel Charteris, a major land and ground rent holder in the Cahir area of County Tipperary. He wanted the practice of holding the Cahir monthly fair on the streets of the town to be abolished and the fair switched to the fair green specifically provided. The practice in Cahir was precisely the same as in Dillon's own town of Ballaghaderreen.

In his reply to Colonel Charteris in January 1951, Dillon, after expressing his thanks for the letter and his apology for a delay in responding, gets down to the issue:

> Will you forgive me if I am quite frank on the subject about which you wrote to me? I know that my view is somewhat unorthodox, but I cannot help feeling that it has some merit to commend it. First, in this regulation-ridden world I have a horror of pushing people about, and having spent most of my life in rural Ireland, I know the irrational passion which small farmers have for showing their stock to what they think is the best advantage. Comparing the background of the street, to what to them seems the vast anonymity of the fair green, they instinctively believe that the former background presents a more flattering setting for the jewels they display. I am told that Hatton Garden diamond merchants would

sooner retire from business than display diamonds on any other background than black velvet, though in the last analysis they know that no skilful jeweller will suffer his judgment to be finally ruled by the first blaze of glory which diamonds on black velvet present. I am afraid that the railings on the square of Cahir are for the small farmers and their modest wares all and more than black velvet is to the merchants of Hatton Gardens.

You rightly surmise that the publicans secretly sympathise with this predilection of the farmers, believing that it brings grist to the mill. I have been 25 years a publican in a small Irish town where the public house has been strategically situated, and I know by experience that this intimate propinquity to the actual buying and selling is not so vitally important as those who enjoy it believe, but it is not a matter of reason, it approximates to atavistic belief, and as St Paul found so often in Corinth and Ephesus, reason without faith was rarely sufficient to overthrow inherited beliefs, however irrational and exotic they may have been.

Lastly, rural Ireland has much of tedium in it, and I am convinced that the monthly fair is for many of our people all that the Place de la Concorde, as one comes out from the Crillon, is for those fortunate enough to have experienced this recurrent delight. I know that I should not stay at the Crillon or indeed go to Paris at all, because I cannot afford the one nor the other, but I do and life would become well nigh intolerable if prudence confined me (which it ought to do) perpetually to the four shores of Ireland. And so, I have never felt myself justified in denying to my neighbours, on the grounds of unanswerable prudence and reason, their irrational joy in displaying their wares everywhere they should not display them; in wasting £15 a month of the ratepayers' money washing streets that they should never have soiled; in glorying in their right to buy from itinerant 'hand-me-downs' the raiment that they should buy from me in the respectable and orderly atmosphere that obtains in my venerable shop.

All this flight from reason seems to me the apotheosis of freedom, and all my annoyance at trying to drive my car through multitudes of bullocks and their proprietors evaporates in the realisation that in your country and mine there are no uniformed representatives of authority to push the people about, but rather that on this day they push me and I push them in friendly but vociferous assertion of exclusive rights which neither of us really have any title to at all.

I hope that this devotion to liberty at the cost of order will not shock you, but I know you will wish me to give you the facts as I see them.

With kind regards and best wishes for 1951 ...

At the time of writing that reply, Dillon was Minister for Agriculture in the first Costello Inter-Party Government: very much a hands-on minister running a major department, a busy man. Then how did he find the time or the inclination, going through his post, to compose what must be one of the most fascinating replies to have emerged from that 'venerable' department? Could it be for real? I first got a copy of it in 1999 from a friend, Eamon McGowan of the wonderfully entitled firm of Sligo solicitors, Argue and Phibbs. So it has done the rounds.

I have no doubt the letter to Colonel Charteris was vintage Dillon. He had a particular genius, as demonstrated daily when the Dáil was sitting and regularly in his political speeches, of being able to respond immediately in perfect phraseology whether or not he had notice of what might be discussed. The colourful allusions and embellishments seemed to come as part of the flow. Listeners would be disappointed if they didn't. I believe it would have been possible for him to have dictated the Charteris reply in the same time it would have taken some others to do a standard 'Dear Constituent' letter already sent out, in one form or another, on so many occasions that it could make it to its destination without the help of the postman.

I must admit, however, that I never could find out if there was anything in particular St Paul (no mean hand at the old letter to constituents himself) did in Corinth or Ephesus to find himself lined up as a Dillon man on the importance of background, whether selling diamonds in Hatton Gardens or bullocks at the monthly fair at Cahir.

Maybe they should bring back the fairs!

Politician at the Typewriter

The young barrister Brian Lenihan had had a satisfactory day in court. He was beginning to build up a steady practice on the Midland Circuit. Soon, however, he would be concentrating on a political career after winning a seat in the Dáil for Fianna Fáil, the traditional party of the family. Uniquely, he won that seat several years before his father, Paddy, made it to the Dáil. With his ability, flamboyance, his special gifts as a communicator and his steadfast refusal to take himself too seriously, Brian Lenihan was destined to become one of the great characters of Irish politics in the second half of the twentieth century.

The Circuit Court on this particular day was sitting in Roscommon town and, after completing his work, Brian walked from the Courthouse in Abbey Street to Tom Greally's pub nearby to meet a good friend, Tom Rennick, editor of *The Longford Leader*, for what they intended to be a quiet drink while Tom tidied up his reports for his paper from the Circuit

Court sittings. *The Longford Leader* was a long-established, traditional-style provincial paper with a history of being strongly supportive of Fine Gael. It was also well known locally that some of the best editorials critical of Fianna Fáil were Tom's work. An incidental matter like that never interfered with the friendship between the two men. It was the same with other such friendships forged throughout Brian's political career. There was no better person to argue the Fianna Fáil case, whether that case was a good one or if it was non-existent. He could never see why fighting your case should mean losing your friends.

In Greally's pub, Brian was soon joined by several of the legal people in town for the Circuit Court sitting. From the decibel level it was obvious that the lawyers' session had taken off very quickly. For Tom, however, things were going in the opposite direction. An urgent phone call had told him of trouble with the printing press in Longford, so all copy was needed immediately. Tom had to complete his court cases and write an editorial. He was a professional and could rattle off an editorial very quickly once he had decided on the subject matter.

When Brian came along to check how work was progressing with his friend, Tom still wasn't happy with any particular topic for the editorial.

'What about the roads?' Brian suggested. 'With the potholes, we'll be lucky to get home. There's bound to be something in that for you. Or what about the farmers? I see they're crying again about the price of cattle.'

Unfortunately, Tom had written editorials on both these subjects in recent weeks. Brian was fully conscious of the time factor and came up with yet another idea for the editorial.

'We all know that Éamon de Valera is coming to Longford for a meeting,' Brian said. 'What about doing your editorial on de Valera and Fianna Fáil, giving them a bit of advice, that kind of stuff? You can't go wrong.'

Tom acknowledged that it would be a good idea under the

circumstances, but there was no way that he, as editor of *The Longford Leader*, would do an editorial on Dev with the clock against him as it now was.

'I'll do it for you,' said Brian.

'Forget it. That's not possible. Brian Lenihan writing the editorial for *The Longford Leader!*'

'No problem,' was the reply from Brian. 'You don't want it good; you want it now.'

In the end it was the deadline back at the office in Longford that made the decision for them. While Tom would finish up what remained to be done on the 'Court copy', Brian would draft out an editorial offensive to nobody. There were a few pages of blank writing paper in a brief he had with him from a case settled earlier in the day.

While Brian confined himself to the general instructions 'to be bland', he couldn't quite resist the opportunity for a bit of devilment and, as he came near the end, was 'having a bit of a go' at his colleagues in Fianna Fáil!

When the job was done, Tom was pleased with the editorial. In places it was pretty strong stuff. Back in the office in Longford, the staff were also pleased, although it has to be said that their primary interest was in filling the hole in the leader page so that they could put it to bed.

In due course, de Valera arrived in Longford. With the passage of time and failing memories, some say there was no meeting at all, but others give a credible account of a sizeable gathering.

At the beginning of his speech Dev dealt with all the essentials, including, of course, partition and the Irish language. He then proceeded to the issues of the day and, coming towards the end, suddenly whipped out from under his black cloak a copy of *The Longford Leader*. Waving it in the air, he told the crowd that he wanted to bring to their attention a scurrilous piece of writing. Many of the readers of this paper were themselves Fianna Fáil supporters and this was an insult to them, he declared. He then went through the editorial paragraph by paragraph and analysed it and dissected it as only de Valera could. This was great stuff for the crowd and they all sensed it was a bit of a bonus.

Watching the performance from his seat on the platform was Brian Lenihan. He was described by one man in the audience as sage-like, though how one so young could manage that is a mystery. He nodded his head vigorously in agreement as Dev made point after point about the editorial.

'Time someone said that,' Brian whispered to his neighbour on the platform. On occasions he was also able to act as a sort of cheerleader. With his very thorough knowledge of the editorial, he knew when the pieces coming up would especially annoy Dev and he was able to encourage the crowd. Not that the crowd at any de Valera meeting needed much encouragement. All that was required to get them in full throttle was a good long pause to let them draw breath. They were happy to shout their heads off for him, but there was a limit!

'Great speech, Chief,' Brian said to Mr de Valera as he prepared to leave.

'Thank you,' said Dev. 'The editorial was a great help.'

On Mature Reflection
— Conor O'Clery

Irish people are said to appreciate eloquence. They relish a colourful turn of phrase, a clever riposte, a wicked insult. They treasure a *bon mot*, a good Malapropism or a splendidly outrageous mixed metaphor. This is one of the few countries where newspapers carry long columns of quotations headed 'This Week They Said'. What makes our phrases and quotations worth recording?

Some illuminate for us aspects of national life and debate. We remember Seán Lemass's comment in 1928 that Fianna Fáil was a 'slightly constitutional party', because it described precisely the party's constitutional role at the time, and many recall George Colley's (now so prescient) warning in 1967 about low standards in high places, because he alone dared voice an unpalatable truth. When Justice Minister Seán MacEoin expressed a fear in 1951 about getting 'a belt of the crozier', the phrase entered our political lexicon because it so aptly described the relationship between politicians and the bishops.

Other quotations betray a certain cast of mind often unique in its Irishness, such as the 1966 comment by Oliver J. Flanagan, TD: 'Sex never came to Ireland until Telifís Éireann went on the air.' Trawling through the history of the country one finds many such examples of unintentionally revealing remarks. We know exactly what UVF leader Billy Mitchell meant when he said in 1975, 'I may be a bad Christian but I'm a good Protestant', and how Joseph Murray, president of the League of Decency, could say in 1974, 'I have received pledges from 2,000 people and two Protestants.'

Some phrases bear out the wisdom of Séamus Heaney's advice: 'Whatever you say, say nothing.' Among them must be numbered Brian Lenihan's 'on mature recollection' which came to signify a changed story. We recall others because we simply enjoy *double entendres* in high places, such as Jack Lynch's 'I would not like to leave contraception on the long finger too long,' or the then Archbishop of Dublin Dr Kevin McNamara's plea for contraceptive legislation to 'be treated as a dead letter'. We hoot with laughter at Margaret Thatcher's farewell compliment to Willie Whitelaw, her former NI Secretary, that 'every prime minister needs a Willie'.

We also delight if the mask slips and we hear what someone really thinks, as when British politician Reginald Maudling was overheard saying as he left Belfast: 'For God's sake bring me a large Scotch. What an awful bloody country!'

Some of the most important phrases of the century are not so well remembered, however. Few people are aware of the crucial words of British prime minister David Lloyd George, when he invited Irish republicans to a conference 'to ascertain how the association of Ireland with the community of nations known as the British Empire can best be reconciled with Irish national aspirations'. This phrase became the foundation of the subsequent Anglo-Irish Treaty, just as the 1990 statement of Northern Ireland Secretary Peter Brooke that 'the British government has no selfish strategic or economic interest in Northern Ireland' became the corner stone of the peace process. (Note that there is no comma after the word 'selfish' which would quite change the meaning.)

Lloyd George cautioned MPs during a debate on the Treaty that 'you do not settle great complicated problems the moment you utter a good phrase about them.' 'Good phrases' have, however, played a unique role in shaping our perceptions of history, and many echoed down through the century. This is especially true of the anti-Home Rule rhetoric used by Edward Carson and others, described by British prime minister Herbert Asquith as a 'reckless rodomontade' which 'furnishes for the future a complete grammar of anarchy'.

How often have modern unionist politicians repeated such catch-cries as Carson's 'Ulster is not for sale'. Republican speechmakers of today also liberally use such emotive quotations as Pádraig Pearse's '…

the fools, the fools, the fools! — they have left us our Fenian dead …' or Terence MacSwiney's '… it is not they who can inflict most, but they who can suffer most, will conquer.' Winston Churchill derided the 'frothings' of the anti-Home Rule mob, suggesting that 'when the worst comes to the worst, we shall find that civil war evaporates in uncivil words.' It was not his only Irish misjudgment. In 1945 we find the UK representative in Dublin, Sir John Maffey, warning Churchill not to take on Éamon de Valera in open debate as 'phrases make history here'.

Literature also supplied many phrases which endured. When the Bishop of Derry, Edward Daly, said despairingly in 1993, 'The gunmen are not dying for the people, the people are dying for the gunmen,' he was quoting almost verbatim from Seán O'Casey's 1923 play *The Shadow of a Gunman*. Fine Gael TD John Kelly caused an uproar in August 1981 for saying the state was [like a sow] 'being rent by a farrow of cannibal piglets', but he was merely taking his cue from James Joyce's Stephen Dedalus, who said 'Ireland is the old sow that eats her farrow.' W.B. Yeats gave many hostages to fortune when he chronicled in verse the emergence of 'a terrible beauty', but also wondered in later life if some words of his might have sent out 'certain men the English shot'.

He was not the first to regret his use of stirring language. In the very first year of the twentieth century John Ingram, author of the ballad 'Who Fears to Speak of '98?', disclaimed any sympathy 'with those who preach sedition in our own day'.

Politicians sometimes rework the phrases of their enemies to fit the needs of the moment. When the prominent unionist David Brewster told colleagues in 1998 that the present Stormont might give unionists 'freedom to achieve freedom', he was mimicking Michael Collins's assurance in 1921 that the Treaty gave not 'ultimate freedom' but the 'freedom to achieve it'.

Likewise when John Hume — who has defined political leadership as being about 'changing the language of others' — defended meeting Sinn Féin by saying 'No stone should be left unturned to advance the cause of peace', he was taking his line from unionist leader James Craig, who justified meeting Michael Collins with the words: 'No stone should be left unturned to try to stop the murdering that is going on in Ireland.' When unionist leader Brian Faulkner wondered aloud after putting his signature to the 1973 Sunningdale Agreement, 'which one of us has signed his own death warrant', he was consciously echoing Collins's best-remembered quotation after signing the 1921 Treaty, 'I may have signed my actual death warrant.' (All the Sunningdale signatories stayed alive except Faulkner, who died in a hunting accident.)

Twenty years ago David Trimble called the new Northern Ireland Assembly 'a pluralist parliament for a pluralist people', in a deliberate reworking of his predecessor James Craig's famous 1934 utterance 'our boast is that we are a Protestant Parliament for a Protestant State.' On another occasion he invoked the unionist election slogans of 1925 to taunt the IRA for refusing to decommission weapons, saying: 'There is a certain irony, is there not, in the IRA's constant litany of "Not an inch" and "What we have we hold!"'

The words 'Not an inch' have dominated the unionist lexicon throughout the [twentieth] century, typically in the Ulster Unionist campaign against the 1985 Anglo-Irish Agreement, and the more recent 'No guns, no government' stance. John Hume remarked once, 'If you took the word "no" out of the English language, all of them would be speechless.' Trimble has warned recently, 'We're perfectly capable, should the need arise, of saying "no", especially if it's going back to what we know best'. He was picking up a controversial remark by Sinn Féin's Francie Molloy, who had threatened that if negotiations failed 'We'd simply go back to what we know best'.

A new grammar of anarchy has been written by Sinn Féin, including Gerry Adams's famous remark about the IRA. 'They haven't gone away, you know.' Danny Morrison's (often misquoted) comment: 'Will anyone here object if, with a ballot paper in this hand, and an armalite in this hand, we take power in Ireland?' It was his version of an 'Irish solution to an Irish problem', the words used by C.J. Haughey to describe his contraceptive legislation in 1979.

If Irish phrases employed to cope with Irish problems cause confusion to outsiders, it is worth remembering the despairing British comment of the 1930s: 'Gladstone spent his declining years trying to guess the answer to the Irish Question; unfortunately when he was getting warm, the Irish secretly changed the question.' But perhaps the best advice for the newcomer to Irish politics was that tendered by Willie Whitelaw. When asked once for his views on Irish history he replied wisely: 'One must be careful not to prejudge the past.'

([Conor O'Clery, 'Whatever you say, on mature recollection, say nothing,' *The Irish Times*, 16 October 1999]. The quotation above and more are listed in chronological order in *Ireland in Quotes: A History of the Century*, published by O'Brien Press.)

'Begob,' said Pee, 'I like your style!'
The December 1993 Summit meeting of EU Heads of

Government had agreed on the doubling of Structural Funds overall. But the doubling of what? The Taoiseach, Albert Reynolds, had translated it into hard euro — it was 8 billion euro for the Irish. Immediately, doubts were cast on his figure. But that was Albert's figure and the man who had to deliver was Minister for Foreign Affairs, Dick Spring.

One way or another, this was it. This would be the last time that the Irish would need to bring their big buckets with them going to the well in Brussels. The culmination came in a night of tough negotiations recalled brilliantly by Fergus Finlay in his book *Snakes & Ladders*. There are no 'High Noons' in Brussels. But who needs one with Irish Commissioner Pee Flynn around.

So there was a lot at stake when we set off for Brussels on 20 July 1994, so much so that an RTÉ crew came to Dublin airport to film our departure. The word from Brussels was that Bruce Millan, an EU Commissioner in charge of Structural Funds, wasn't prepared to agree to a penny more than 6 billion. Ireland was going to have to capitulate.

Dick's officials were worried. They had done remarkable, even heroic work in maintaining Ireland's case. But now it was down to a political decision.

The team was led throughout those negotiations by Noel Fahey, the Department's assistant secretary in charge of economic policy, and Pádhraic McKiernan, Ireland's Permanent Representative in Brussels. They were as different as chalk and cheese — Noel with a permanently worried air, always surrounded by reams of paper, and Pádhraic who created the impression almost of a conspirator, who would glide people into corners and emerge with another favour granted for his country.

But they were an incredible team — both men of

powerful intellect and an unparalleled knowledge of the European institutions and their methods. They were assisted by David Cooney, another extraordinary young diplomat who went on to play a remarkable role in the peace process.

On this occasion, because of the high stakes, the team was augmented by a senior official from the Department of Finance, Michael Tutty, who had constructed a good deal of the mathematical calculations we were relying on. Paddy Teahon, the secretary of the Department of the Taoiseach, joined us to keep a watching brief on behalf of his political boss, and also to twist any arms he could find (Paddy has an amazingly pleasant way of doing that). It couldn't get any more high-powered — even though we all felt it wasn't really necessary for the Department of Finance to be riding shotgun on us.

It culminated in a long night of tough negotiation — and an incredible performance by Pádraig Flynn, Ireland's unique Commissioner, who, immediately on our arrival, appointed himself as mediator between the Irish and the rest of Europe. It was the first time I ever saw him in action, and it was an unforgettable sight.

EU negotiations are like no other. Mostly you sit crowded together in a small room, the Minister and his entourage, without food, coffee or even drinkable water, waiting for developments, while officials scurry backwards and forwards among the participants.

On this particular night, it was Pee Flynn who had given himself the job of scurrying, and it was us who had to sit and wait. Occasionally, action and decision would be called for — and then speed was crucial.

'D'ye know what rough trade is, lads?' was Flynn's opening gambit. 'Because ye're in for a lot of it tonight!'

We had an idea what rough trade was — not something you'd normally associate with genteel negotiations over the share-out of structural funds. Dick Spring knew that it meant a ruthless ganging up on the hapless Foreign Minister who was holding out against the rest, and he made his first crucial decision of the night, by asking Flynn to arrange for the other Ministers to gather in their meeting room upstairs.

I didn't go up for the impromptu speech he made to the other fourteen, but Noel Fahey did. When he came back down, they were all a bit tense. Dick had told his Ministerial colleagues, in no uncertain terms, that rough trade wasn't going to work. He would stay as long as necessary, and wasn't going to be either bent or broken. If they wanted the matter resolved, they knew what it would take.

When Dick left the room for a minute Noel Fahey turned to me.

'Now I know what it's like to be lining out for a tough match with Spring as captain,' he said. 'And I'm glad I'm on our team.'

That was around eleven o'clock. For the next six hours Dick Spring disappeared from time to time, as a relatively friendly sighting was made in the corridor, to catch people on a one-to-one basis and gradually build a base of support.

The rest of us sat, occasionally being given a new set of figures to work on, and a new version of Pee Flynn in full flight.

In the late evening Michael Tutty came to see Dick. He explained that he had an exam the following morning in Dublin which would be one of the final stages in a master's degree. He wondered how the Tánaiste would feel if he made a dash to the airport to catch the last flight home.

'I wouldn't ask normally, Tánaiste,' he said, 'but it's clear that nothing is going to happen tonight, and I won't be needed to do any calculations.'

Dick looked at him coolly, and asked what use the master's degree would be to him after Michael's transfer to Cavan. It was Michael's first exposure to Dick's sense of humour, and he nearly had to be picked off the floor. When he was reassured by Dick for the third time that it was only a joke, and that he could go home and sit the exam (which he subsequently passed with flying colours), I was left in charge of the calculator, to my horror.

Every now and again Commissioner Flynn would make a grand entrance to our room, to give a progress report, always in the most flamboyant language possible. After one of his eruptions, and when he had swept out again, I heard one of our senior diplomats murmur, 'I've lost him surely — I've lost the only playboy of the western world!'

In the course of the night I gradually became familiar with hitherto alien concepts like mecu and becu. All the figures we had to use were in millions and billions of ECU in 1992 prices, and as the man with the calculator, it was my job to convert them into Irish pounds at current value. By the end of the night I knew the formula by heart.

Eventually Pee Flynn burst in again. He sat beside me and slapped me on the knee.

'Quick!' he said. 'Quick! 9.2 becu — '92 prices. What is it? Quick!'

I was unnerved by the intensity of this apparition, as I suppose I was meant to be. But I still managed to tap the figures into the calculator, and after checking it a few times, discovered that we had now got to £7.85

billion — as close to our target as made no difference. We all agreed.

'I'll tell you what you do now, Dick,' said Pee. 'You ring Albert, and tell him it's our judgment that's the best we're going to do, and ask his permission to shake hands.'

'I don't think so,' Dick replied. 'I'll ring Albert and tell him we've taken it as far as we can. But if I think it's a fair deal, I'm not going to be asking permission to shake hands.'

'Begob,' said Pee, 'I like your style!'

It was now five in the morning. After Dick rang the Taoiseach at home in Dublin and told him what he was going to do, I was put on the phone to give him the exact figures.

It was the first time that I was exposed to Albert Reynolds' sharpness and alertness. It was five in the morning, and we had just been through one of the longest and roughest days I ever remember. I had been working with a set of figures all night, and he had just woken from his bed in Dublin. At least, I assume he had been asleep — maybe he'd stayed up to wait for the call. As I was to discover later, he thought little of staying awake all night if necessary.

But he quizzed me backwards and forwards, asking me to recite the conversion formula that had been used, and apparently checking it against a formula he had developed himself, before pronouncing himself satisfied that at least the arithmetic was right. 'Good man,' he said, before going back to sleep: the sleep of the just. You wouldn't think that this was a deal that might make or break his reputation.

The only thing left to do was to shake hands with Jacques Delors. Dick wanted a witness to the transaction — because there'd be nothing in writing. The Commissioner stepped forward.

'The Tánaiste may not be of My Party,' he announced. 'But he's Tánaiste of My Country. Commissioner Pee Flynn will be proud to be his witness.'

Immediately Joe Brennan, the Commissioner's *Chef de Cabinet*, leaned forward and whispered urgently in his ear. Commissioner Flynn spoke again, his tone if anything more dramatic than a moment previously.

'Commissioner Pee Flynn cannot do what he just said he would do,' he announced grandly, and as if we should have known what he was going to say.

'The Commissioner has taken an oath that precludes him from bearing witness on behalf of a member state. Ye had better get yourselves another witness!'

And he swept out of the room, like Anew McMaster on a bad night.

Dick went and shook hands with Jacques Delors — witnessed by Paddy McKiernan and Paddy Teahon — and the night of the 8 billion was over.

We were to get a *fourchette* — and its upper limit would be the 7.85 billion that was agreed. A *fourchette*, we all decided, was a two-pronged fork in French, and there was no doubt in our minds that we'd get the higher prong.

A couple of days later when I was drafting something for the Tánaiste's speech to the Dáil about the occasion, I fell to wondering whether there was an English equivalent to the word *fourchette*. I looked it up in the dictionary, and there indeed it was (and is — page 465 of the Concise Oxford Dictionary, 1992 edition): 'a thin fold of skin at the back of the vulva'. I decided to leave it out of the Tánaiste's speech!

It taught me a lot, that night — about standing your ground, about how to build a solid support from nothing, about how to make a judgment call and act on it. They were the things Dick Spring did, and he never put a foot wrong. Albert Reynolds trusted him that night, and didn't interfere — but he was sharp and totally in touch. These were two men who knew their objectives, who knew how to get there, and who respected each other's toughness and judgment. There were bound to make a great team, despite everything.

And they would need to, with some of the other things that were going on.

[Fergus Finlay, *Snakes & Ladders*, New Island, 1998]

5. The Ones who Broke the Mould

Eddie Kelly

The first introduction I had to politicians working, or more accurately talking, was reporting on meetings of Monaghan County Council for *The Monaghan Argus* newspaper in the early 1950s. Amongst the councillors at the time was Eddie Kelly, a publican, from Essexfort, Carrickmacross.

Since then, as a journalist, and later as a politician, I have met a fair share of our Dáil deputies, senators and county councillors — some of them in all three incarnations. But to this day, Eddie Kelly remains for me a man unmatched in any of the County Halls.

He may not ever have got to run the country, like Jackie Healy-Rae did for a while, or even gain for himself a national profile, but, to borrow a couple of words from Patrick Kavanagh, his near neighbour in Mucker and Inniskeen, Eddie Kelly, from his very entry into politics, was never destined to be an 'anonymous performer'.

His first election was for the Carrickmacross District Board of Guardians. At that time in Irish politics, among the most damaging things that could be said about you was that you were a 'turncoat' or a 'twister'. Even to this day, it's still not a helpful designation, despite the country being more or less permanently ruled through made marriages. Eddie Kelly's problem was that, although he was a very young man who was only starting off in politics, adversaries were already levelling accusations at him.

He decided to take them head-on as he cycled around on his canvass or spoke from the back of a cart at the fair in Carrickmacross or from a presbytery chair outside the church gates.

Central to Eddie's campaign was a poster he had designed and produced himself. The picture was of a smiling Eddie with his coat turned inside out twisting the starting handle of a tractor. His campaign slogan was 'Vote for Eddie, the Twister'. He headed the poll.

His next election was for Monaghan County Council. Again he won a seat and continued to win it at nearly every council election until his retirement. For seventeen of these years, he was Chairman of Monaghan Council. At the annual vote for the chair, he was regularly opposed by his own Fianna Fáil party, but supported by Fine Gael and the Protestant Association Party. Sometimes he was elected by his own casting vote since the Council was usually — and conveniently — evenly divided.

In 1954 Eddie Kelly was elected a Dáil deputy for Monaghan, along with Erskine Childers for Fianna Fáil. At the next election, however, he failed to get a Fianna Fáil nomination to run again, at the convention in Ballybay. For most politicians, that would have been it. Not for Eddie. On the next Sunday he attended the Fine Gael convention in Carrickmacross, sought and got a Fine Gael nomination and contested the 1957 general election as no less than the running mate of James Dillon, the leader of the party. He didn't quite make it, but there wasn't much in it. Transfers went wrong.

Afterwards Eddie took his defeat at the polls with his usual good grace and charm. 'It would have been interesting to have sat on both sides of the House,' he told me. 'I think the people of Monaghan liked my brand of consistency.'

P. J. Lindsay

Patrick J. Lindsay came from the townland of Doolough, near Geesala, in north Mayo, a townland that was to produce three Dáil deputies from three separate families.

Lindsay himself first stood in the 1937 general election as a Fine Gael candidate while still at University College, Galway, studying philosophy, Latin and Greek. Already he had a reputation as a brilliant public speaker, but you needed more than that to make it to the Dáil. They loved the spouting and the heckling at the church gates and at the fairs in north Mayo, and Lindsay was the very best. But above all in those hungry times, they wanted their Dáil deputies living locally to be available on demand; this was not too easy for Lindsay, living in Dublin and working first as a teacher and later building up a busy law practice. He made it to the Dáil in 1954 after persistently trying in every election, and soon became Minister for the Gaeltacht in John A. Costello's second National Coalition government.

It was a pleasant drive up to Áras an Úachtaráin to collect his seal of office from the President, but unfortunately for Pat Lindsay, the government fell after a few years and, while he retained his Dáil seat, Minister Lindsay and the other ministers had to head back to the Park. The mood is described by himself in his memoir, *Memories*:

> When the new Dáil met de Valera was elected Taoiseach for the last time. His party won 77 seats in the election and all we had to look forward to was a lengthy stay in opposition backed by a depressed and demoralised Party.
>
> In some ways our situation is best summed up by an incident that happened after the defeat of Jack

Costello as Taoiseach. We immediately headed back, as was the case in those days, to return our Seals of Office (or as I called them, our Sodality Medals) to the President, Seán T. O'Kelly, at Áras an Úachtaráin. I have to say his manner towards us was quite different to what it had been the previous time. On that occasion he gave us a drink; this time he did not. It was a bleak day.

But in any event we drove down the Quays on McBirney's side, '40 paces from O'Connell Bridge' as the old ad. used to say. I was sitting in the back of the ministerial Dodge, right behind the driver, the late Sergeant Paddy Byrne. Sitting beside him was the secretary of the Government, Maurice Moynihan. In the back of the car, in the middle, was Jack Costello with his head down and looking totally unlike the kind of man he was — he looked gruff whereas he was the kindest of men. On his left was James Dillon and, as we passed the old Irish House, a public house with figurines outside it — it's gone now as a result of the Wood Quay fiasco — James Dillon said: 'You know, I never fail to be intrigued by the old Irish House.'

'If you saw it four times a day coming from the Four Courts,' said Costello, 'you wouldn't be a bit impressed.'

The conversation continued with James Dillon saying, 'You know I was never in a public house in my life except my own in Ballaghadereen, which I sold because when I saw people going home having spent so much money on drink, I decided that they were depriving their families of the essentials.' To my consternation, Jack Costello said that he was in a public house only once in his life, in Terenure, and was nearly choked by a bottle of orange. I was totally appalled by this state of affairs and I expressed my feelings as follows:

'******, I know why we are driving in this direction and why we are out of touch with the people.'

For we were out of touch. The public house is the countryman's club, where everything is discussed and where contacts are made. And here was a Prime Minister of an agricultural country, in a public house only once in his life, and a Minister for Agriculture, who was responsible for brewing and distilling, had never been in a public house except for his own. How could we be going in any other direction?

[Patrick Lindsay, *Memories*, Blackwater Press, 1992]

Tull MacAdoo

My favourite TD, Deputy Tull MacAdoo (writer of *Letters of a Successful TD*), missed out on being born. But that was about the last thing he missed. He was a wholly unconstitutional TD created by John B. Keane, but manifesting many of the characteristics, admirable and otherwise, of TDs who arrived in Leinster House in the orthodox way through the ballot box. That's what makes Tull so intriguing and also deserving of close study, as used to be recommended by Dr Basil Chubb, Professor of Political Science at Trinity College, Dublin. John B. himself wanted to ensure that latecomers to Tull fully appreciated his wide range of talents and the potential still there. He did this by way of a special introduction in *Letters of an Irish Minister of State*.

I address this introduction to readers who may not be familiar with the exploits of Tull MacAdoo TD. We saw how Tull silenced his arch-rival, schoolmaster James Flannery by unorthodox methods. Flannery would have the general public believe that the now-famous battle of Glenalee never took place. Flannery in fact claimed that the entire affair, in which Tull single-handedly killed one black and tan and wounded several others, was purely a figment of Tull's imagination. The following is a statement which Flannery had published in a newspaper known as *The Demoglobe*.

Mr James Flannery NT asserts that he has conclusive proof that there was never a battle of Glenalee. In an exclusive interview Mr Flannery told our reporter that there may have been a few scraps there between weasels and rabbits but there was no gun battle.

'There were battles', he said, 'between weasels and rabbits and murder was perpetrated when a sparrow-hawk assaulted a wren.' He said, 'the battle was a figment of the imagination of Mr Tull MacAdoo TD.' He challenged Mr MacAdoo to refute his statement.

'I am convinced', Mr Flannery concluded, 'that no battle was ever fought there and', he added, 'I have the evidence to prove it.' Whether he had or not we shall never know for shortly afterwards Flannery went back on his statement. It appears that in his prime he (Flannery) sired a daughter through the good offices of one Jenny Jordan, of Crabapple Hill. Tull MacAdoo informed the ultra-respectable teacher that he would be obliged to reveal the existence of the illegitimate daughter, who was called Maud, after Maud Gonne, unless Flannery perform-ed a complete about-turn and published a retraction. This the schoolmaster was obliged to do in view of Tull's threat to expose him.

Almost immediately there was a general election in which Tull secured the largest personal vote ever recorded in the constituency. His surplus guaranteed

the election of his running mate Dan Stack, a feat
which endeared him to his party boss and Taoiseach
of the country, Mr Lycos. Tull had more than one
close friend in the cabinet but perhaps his most
influential was the Minister for Continental
Relations, Mr James McFillen, who also happened to
be godfather to Tull's daughter Kate.

One morning after a cabinet meeting McFillen
called the Taoiseach aside and informed him that he
was proposing Tull MacAdoo for the post of minister
of state. At first the Taoiseach laughed but when there
was no responding laugh he turned serious and said:

'I like poor old Tull. In fact there's nobody I like
more and I happen to know that his loyalty is above
question.'

McFillen seized his chance. The conversation was
taking a direction which appealed to him. It was a
time when the loyalty of some of the party's oldest
members left a lot to be desired.

'Loyalty should be worth something,' McFillen said
and waited lest any further utterance of his might
compromise the gambit. The Taoiseach tweaked his
upper lip as was his wont when he was giving his
undivided attention to the question in hand.

'But what is there for him?' he asked. 'He lacks the
education. He's not the most literate of men and he
has yet to make his maiden speech after thirty years.'

McFillen waited. The Taoiseach, he sensed, was
addressing the question to himself. A long silence
followed.

'Isn't there a danger', the Taoiseach asked, 'that he
might embarrass us?'

'In what way?' McFillen replied innocently.

'He is what certain academics on the opposition
benches would call an ignorant man.'

'Forgive me, my dear Lionel, but they've called you worse.'

'Touché,' said the Taoiseach, 'but let's face it, poor old Tull is a born backbencher. He lacks the poise, the confidence and we both know he's anything but articulate.'

'That could be a blessing,' McFillen put in, knowing the Taoiseach's abhorrence of effusiveness and long-windedness.

'You're scoring heavily, Mac,' the leader said, 'but there is the danger he may make a show of himself and leave us down with a bang. Have you thought of that?'

'I've thought of everything. By the way, the one thing he'd never do is let us down. He has intelligence and infinite cunning and he has a daughter who manages him most astutely from the wings.'

'I know all about the daughter.' The Taoiseach relapsed into silence. McFillen knew that Lycos had made up his mind.

'What would you say, Mac', said he, 'to Minister for State for Bog Land Areas?'

'I would love it,' McFillen answered, 'although it seems a bit bare.'

'Alright,' said the Taoiseach, tweaking his upper lip a second time, 'how about Minister for Bog Land Areas with Special Responsibilities for Game and Wildlife?'

'Beautiful, absolutely beautiful.' McFillen's appreciation was genuine. 'The greater the number of words after his name the better,' he said. 'This will really impress his constituents. There will be bonfires in Kilnavarna when the announcement is made.'

So it was that Tull MacAdoo became a Minister of State. The Taoiseach need not have worried. Tull was a man of few words and if these were not always well chosen they were, at least, positively harmless. He opened every speech with a sentence in Gaelic: *Cuirim fáilte romhaimh go léir, a chairde* and ended every speech with: May God bless ye all now and leave ye in good health! His daughter put the meat in the sandwich so to speak.

[That extract from *The Celebrated Letters of John B. Keane* Vol. 1, Mercier Press, 1996, is reprinted by kind permission of Mary Keane, a great lady I first met in the pub in Listowel in the mid-1960s. We were filming for RTÉ, a short piece on Sonny Canavan relating to his rather unusual habit of taking out his glass eye and leaving it on the table at home, 'for general observation purposes', while he went into Listowel for a pint.]

Joe Leneghan

Joe Leneghan from Belmullet, Co. Mayo, was an Independent Dáil deputy for North Mayo from 1954 to 1957. Because of his support for the Lemass government of the time (a majority of minus one was the Taoiseach's own description of his voting situation) in seeing through the Dáil the turnover tax legislation, he became known as Turnover Joe, a name he frequently used himself by way of introduction at his fair day speeches.

Leneghan was a robust debater, especially at Mayo County Council meetings where he dominated, amazed, and frequently amused for many years. Occasionally he took part in Dáil debates, but more in the crossfire than in the hard slog of the Committee stage. 'You're up and down like a whore's knickers' (often attributed to Emmet) was one of his more famous interventions when he felt that an Opposition spokesman was intervening too often for his liking in the discussions in the House.

Michael Finlan, then Western correspondent of *The Irish Times*, was reporting on a Mayo County Council meeting shortly before the November 1975 by-election that brought the current Fine Gael leader, Enda Kenny, to Dáil Éireann. When Joe Leneghan had made enough headlines to keep all the Mayo newspapers going for a week, he retired to the nearby Imperial Hotel, followed shortly by Michael Finlan and other members of the press corps and a few of the councillors who did not have to chase up constituency work in the County Council offices. Soon Joe Leneghan, as was the custom, was regaling them, this time with the story of a remarkable midwife who operated in the Castlebar area and a broad hinterland around.

'Arrah I'll tell you,' said Joe Leneghan, 'there was this midwife who had to travel miles all over west Mayo on her bike delivering babies. She was kept very busy, for sure. Between the lot of us, she didn't have a moment's rest, but she was out night and day trying to keep up. She did some notable maternity work that should put her into the history books. Sure, wasn't it her who brought meself into the world? And that wasn't all. She was there at the bed to deliver Henry Kenny, Enda's father, when he was born. That wasn't the end of her work either. She had to cycle like hell to get to the bed in time when another man, who was destined for fame, was born in Castlebar. The man she delivered on that occasion was none other than Charles Haughey. So there you have it. This very busy midwife was responsible for bringing into the world meself, Henry Kenny and Charlie Haughey … and any woman who did that has a lot to answer for.'

Gerry Fitt
Gerry Fitt, who died in August 2005, was a co-founder and first leader of the Social, Democratic and Labour Party (SDLP). He was one of the major political figures in Northern Ireland during the 1970s and early 1980s and led the SDLP in the power-sharing government with Unionists after the 1974 Sunningdale Agreement.

Amongst the tributes at Gerry Fitt's funeral service in Westminster Cathedral was one by journalist Chris Ryder, Gerry's great friend. He recalled Lord Fitt's lighter side:

I was with Gerry one day, soon after he was elevated to the House of Lords, when a policeman guarding the opulent corridors stopped him to say there was an urgent message at the central lobby. At the next gateway, another policeman advised that a messenger was roaming the corridors looking for him. 'Tell him I'm on my way to the Terrace Bar,' said Gerry.

Soon afterwards, as we were savouring the first gin of the day, the courier tracked him down and proffered a large embossed envelope. 'My Lord,' he said deferentially as he handed it over.

Gerry was meanwhile fumbling in his inside pocket from where he produced a scrap of paper. 'Can you look after that for me?' he said, pressing it into the messenger's hand.

'Certainly, My Lord.'

After the man had left, Gerry opened the envelope. I watched, expecting a great missive of state to tumble out, but all he extracted was a bundle of grubby banknotes and a handful of coins — his previous day's winnings on the horses, he explained. The scrap of paper was his follow-up bet for that day. Backing horses was, of course, one of Gerry's enduring enjoyments and when he was in residence at his beloved cottage in Murlough Bay, he had an equally deft arrangement with the postman and his bookie in Ballycastle to facilitate his daily wagering.

This was the real Gerry Fitt for, despite his historic personal and political achievements, he never adopted great airs and graces or lost touch with the culture and values of his humble working-class origins in Belfast. No day would have been complete without a string of bets. And then there was his epic capacity for gin.

What singled him out from his contemporaries was his singular political ability, addiction to the associated gossip, a huge talent as a side-splitting raconteur and mimic, and an ingrained humanity....

No cry for help was ever turned away. Even when, after one of his collapses at Stormont, the ambulance man sought his assistance with a problem. 'Put a note in my pocket and I'll call you when I get better,' said a semi-conscious but ever obliging Gerry.

Above all, those closest to him will miss his humour, mischief and jokes. There was the memorable night when he persuaded a British Airways crew to squeeze him on the last flight to Belfast in the only available space — the jump seat in the cockpit — and when he emerged through the door in mid-flight to visit the lavatory, there, in the front row, was an astonished Rev. Ian Paisley. 'Don't worry. I've left it on automatic pilot,' he told his great political rival as he pushed past.

During a stay in Belfast's Royal Victoria Hospital after one bout of illness, Gerry quizzed the nurse caring for him about the origin of the blood that was being pumped into him. 'What do you want to know that for?' she asked. 'We never record anything like that.'

'It must be Prod blood,' he said. 'I feel a terrible urge to sing "The Sash My Father Wore".'

And there was the time when he was staying at Murlough that he persuaded an accomplished young violinist to serenade several of his daughters over the telephone. 'I've been practising my own violin since I came over here,' he lied to them before laughing. Although he mastered the mouth-organ during his days at sea, Gerry never did become the ship's captain or virtuoso violinist that he secretly aspired to be. Instead, after his time at sea, he opted for a life in politics.

Throughout, he set his compass to the great values of social justice, tolerance and reconciliation, and his course never wavered. He worked tirelessly for his constituents and anyone else who asked him, regardless of whether they were Catholic, Protestant or Dissenter, Unionist or Nationalist. His raw courage in the face of intimidation and violence is already legendary, but the violent backdrop to his life and work dismayed and disappointed him. He felt betrayed by those who did not share his unambiguous and unequivocal opposition to violence and terrorism.

Gerry was no saint, but his religious faith was strong, despite being tempered with a degree of superstition. For years, we could never get him to make a will lest it would tempt Providence. Like many old sailors, he always carried, in what he described as 'my arse pocket', a little collection of talismans, which included a half-crown given to him as a donation in his first successful election campaign, several mementoes of his beloved Ann, and a collection of religious medals. These were the authentic pointers to his deep, underlying faith, although at times it wobbled. In recent years, despite the hundreds of flights he had made between Belfast and London, he became increasingly apprehensive about air travel, especially in winter and bad weather. 'I'm always a better Catholic at 30,000 feet,' he would say.

From time to time, especially in the midnight isolation of the cottage at Murlough, he would suffer doubt and distress that he would never see Ann again, but then as the dawn of the new day came spectacularly up over the Mull of Kintyre, he would brighten up and reaffirm his customary faith and confidence that one day they would indeed be reunited in Heaven.

Of his other great passion, the cause of social justice and peace in Ireland, he would equally frequently despair. 'There'll be no peace in Ireland until God sees Fitt,' he would say. Well God has seen Fitt and we can only imagine the hullabaloo he's already causing in Heaven. And when true and lasting peace does come to Ireland, as it will, history must properly credit Gerry Fitt for his great courage and his unrivalled and visionary contribution to the process.

Charlie Haughey

Charlie Haughey liked to be photographed with a cup of tea on informal occasions. Posing for a photographer in his constituency headquarters in Dublin in the 1980s, he asked for a cup of tea. A constituency activist, knowing that it was for photographic purposes, emerged with an empty cup and saucer. Charlie looked at the empty cup and remarked: 'Can you spare it?'

The constituency activist went back to the kitchenette and returned with a cup full of tea as well as two biscuits. Charlie handed back the biscuits and sipped the cup of tea for the photograph, which was published in *The Irish Times* the following day.

Charlie also liked to compose and recite a poem for some social occasions, particularly when he officially opened the Festival of Kerry in Tralee at the end of August. Such was his poetic flourish on one occasion that the then Labour leader, Dick Spring, remarked, 'He has gone from bad to verse!'

[As told by Michael O'Regan, Parliamentary correspondent of *The Irish Times* and regular contributor to *The Vincent Browne Show* when on RTÉ 1 radio.]

———

The Taoiseach Charles J. Haughey had in his diary a brief early morning meeting with two of his Fianna Fáil Dáil deputies. As was usual with these early morning meetings, this one would be held in the Taoiseach's office on the second floor of Government Buildings.

The reason for the meeting or who exactly arranged it in the first place has never become fully clear. However, it can be assumed with certainty that it was not with a view to offering the deputies promotion or anything like that. Indeed, it seems that, despite the special meeting, the two men in question were not amongst the Taoiseach's favourite people.

The most likely reason appears to be that the deputies were under severe pressure from their own constituencies on some issue of importance locally, and that they in turn had put the Taoiseach under pressure to meet them. In matters like this, the outcome, even if it is total failure, can be of less importance than the holding of the meeting with the Taoiseach. The deputies back in the constituencies can tell how they forced the great man to come to the table.

After the allocated time (very short) had been reached, the Taoiseach simply resumed his reading of official documents. Apparently, it was not unusual for him to terminate meetings in that fashion.

The deputies were a bit flustered. They were in a room they had not been in before, in an office different in style from all others (the special ornate panelling was one of the features).

They could not find their way out. After a few failed attempts, one of the deputies plucked up his courage and interrupted Mr Haughey.

Deputy: 'Excuse me, Taoiseach, we're stuck. Could you tell us where's the exit door?'

Taoiseach: 'What's wrong with the window?'

6. The Subtle Art of Debating

Shannon Rabbits

Although first delivered in Dáil Éireann sixty years ago, the forecast of James Dillon (Fine Gael) that the rabbits and not aeroplanes would be making use of the runways at Shannon, it can still be heard the odd time from the Fianna Fáil benches in crossfire in the Chamber.

The background was that in 1947 the Fianna Fáil government had proposals for the development of Shannon (then known as Rineanna). James Dillon was broadly in favour. Another government decision to establish a short-wave radio station that would make it possible to broadcast directly from Ireland to the United States he totally opposed, although the equipment had already been purchased.

Dealing with both issues in the Dáil, in the one sentence he made his famous forecast: 'I venture to swear that five years from today, when the rabbits start playing leapfrog below in Rineanna, the masts which are to direct the radio to the US will be converted into knitting machines to knit the wool of the rabbits from Rineanna.' These are the actual words used by Deputy James Dillon, but they are often misquoted.

Minister for Plumbing

The Dáil was debating the very serious outbreak of foot and mouth disease amongst the cattle herds in England, with the obvious danger of its spreading to Ireland.

The efforts to prevent such a spread were headed by Joe Walsh, Minister for Agriculture, and Noel Davern, Minister of State at the Department. They were generally praised and finally successful. When the campaign was debated in the Dáil, Noel Davern, who was answering Dáil questions for the government, was coming under considerable pressure about what the Opposition claimed were the inadequate precautions and facilities at Dublin airport, especially as regards the disinfecting mats and the footbaths. As the then deputy Louis J. Belton recalled, Noel got a bit annoyed and decided to let the Opposition know the score.

'Who do you think I am? I am not the plumber at Dublin airport,' he said. He was the junior Minister and quite proud to be so and of the job they were doing.

Louis J. Belton: 'We know you are not the plumber, but you are the assistant plumber!'

Hen House Treatment

'A Minister for Agriculture who would make such a ridiculous bargain in Trade Talks deserves to be chained under a hen house for at least twelve hours so as to be able to find out what the hens think of him.'

It may have been the same deputy who described one of his colleagues as a 'dual purpose deputy who kicks the Government with his tongue and in the division Lobby kisses the Government with his feet'.

[From Dáil Report of 1950]

Conscience
— Pat Rabbitte

During the Rainbow Coalition days, the Dáil was scheduled to complete a lengthy debate on some contentious matter or other. Dick Spring, leader of the Labour Party and Tánaiste, was known to be winging his way back from the United States to Baldonnel in time to close the debate on behalf of the government. Labour deputy Seán Ryan was addressing the House and a far-from-happy-looking Brian Cowen, as a front-bench spokesman, was on the Fianna Fáil bench, and having great difficulty containing himself. He finally muttered something to Deputy Ryan to the effect that the Labour Party was once again struggling with its conscience, to which Ryan, wisely or unwisely, replied: 'Well, at least we have a conscience.'

Cowen looked at his watch and said: 'Oh yeah! What time is it landing?'

[Deputy Pat Rabbitte represents Dublin South-West and is a former leader of the Labour Party.]

Political Derby

Anyone who attended Dáil Éireann when Charles J. Haughey and Frank Cluskey were members, especially when they were leaders of their respective parties, could never mistake them for friends. If what they said of each other across the floor of the House often sounded insulting, that was what it was. And naturally there was no question of sympathy from the Labour leader when Minister Haughey returned to the Dáil after a fall from a horse that made it impossible for him to deliver his Budget speech. It was hassle all the way from Cluskey, provoking Haughey into accusing him of dishonest politics, trying to ride two horses at the same time.

Cluskey's immediate response was: 'The Minister can rest assured that this deputy will not fall off either horse!'

Tony Gregory

The Tony Gregory deal was new territory in Irish politics. The man who wanted to carry on as Taoiseach, but who was short of votes, was giving the Independent TD what he asked for his patch in Dublin's north inner city.

Tony Gregory, the Independent representing Dublin North-Central, heard Charles J. Haughey put all the details on the record of the Dáil. Then he made his own lengthy contribution, further stitching in the deal on the records.

'There is just one more point I have to add,' Deputy Gregory concluded.

'Yes,' said David Maloney (Tipperary North), sitting in the Dáil for the first time, 'the rest of the country.'

FÁS

Dáil Deputy Michael Ring (Fine Gael, Mayo) was not too pleased with the announcement that Fianna Fáil and Labour whips had made an agreement which would mean that the Taoiseach, Bertie Ahern, no longer had an obligation to be in the Dáil every Thursday.

'What he was doing', said Deputy Ring, 'was trying to turn the leadership of the country into a FÁS job, one week off and one week on!'

United Nations

It was the day the Irish won full membership of the Security Council of the United Nations in 1980. Congratulations came from all round on the victory and also on the classic campaign the Irish had run.

On the same day John Kelly (Fine Gael, Dublin South-East) was speaking in Dáil Éireann and had availed of the opportunity to pass on his good wishes and his congratulations on the achievement. He then went on to pay a personal tribute to the work of his good friend, Foreign Minister Brian Lenihan.

'However,' he said, 'there is one reservation. I cannot help but think that the world is that little bit less safe than it was a few hours ago!'

7. All in a Day's Work

Footbridge

Long before he became a Dáil deputy, Patrick we'll call him, wanted a footbridge across the river in his home town, where it would shorten the journeys of a lot of people. Some would claim that his bridge campaign might very well have been responsible for shortening his own journey to Leinster House. Certainly it helped. Now it was an embarrassment as he passed the area where the bridge should be, when about his constituency work. But he wasn't as easy to embarrass nowadays as he used to be. He still even talked at branch meetings about the need for the bridge and occasionally raised it on the adjournment of the Dáil. He became a Minister of State and he talked a little less about how important the bridge was in the scale of things. In due course he became a Minister, and he never talked about the bridge.

This was too much for a young councillor of his own party. With his knowledge and passion and presentation of constituency problems, this young fellow reminded Patrick a little of himself on the way up.

'Tell me this, now that you're a Minister, when are you going to actually deliver on your footbridge?' the councillor asked him at a district meeting in what was their first head-to-head clash.

The Minister looked the councillor in the eye. 'Do you mean to tell me,' he asked, 'that they haven't built it yet?'

First round to the Minister!

Is He One of Ours?

One of Pat Lindsay's friends and political workers was Tony Chambers of Newport, County Mayo, who became something of a celebrity himself with his role as a band leader in Pat O'Connor's television adaptation of William Trevor's short story *The Ballroom of Romance*. On election days his first target vote was always a protestant lady who lived on her own in a big farmhouse. Not a certain Fine Gael vote, a waverer, but Tony Chambers always believed in his powers of persuasion. If he got to her house early, the vote was as good as in the bag for his man, and that kind of uncertain vote would sometimes be as good as two votes. Not only would he have copped the vote for Lindsay, he would have kept it away from Lindsay's opponents, whether of the opposition parties or of his own party.

At one particular general election when Tony arrived at the house, he was disappointed that the lady wasn't dressed up as usual for the trip to the polling station. She had her bib (apron) on and was out in the yard feeding the cats.

'I don't think I'll bother going at all this time,' she told a surprised Tony. 'Sure, what's the point?'

Tony was at a loss to know what this lack of interest might be about, but he got a feeling that it was because there was no candidate from her own religion on the ballot paper. He took a mock ballot paper from his pocket. He went down the list carefully until he came to Lindsay. In north Mayo you couldn't be too sure of a name like that.

'What about your man?' Tony asked.

'Is he one of ours?'

Tony didn't say yes or he didn't say no.

'Get your coat, ma'am. Get your coat,' he said, heading for the car.

'Give 'em Hell'

All his colleagues in Dublin City Council and in the Dáil were pleased when Eugene Timmons was elected Lord Mayor of Dublin for the second time. Here surely was the quiet man of Irish politics, never raising his voice above what would be to others a whisper, never getting involved in the routine arguments of politics, and never the harsh word.

By contrast, his good friend Joe Dowling (Fianna Fáil, Dublin/Ballyfermot) seemed to relish confrontation with the Opposition and for this purpose he was lucky to have a voice made as if for the old Hill 16 in Croke Park, in the days when Dublin were winning All-Irelands.

Both men were sent down by Fianna Fáil headquarters to work the Dunhill area of Waterford during a by-election. It was Eugene's turn to speak outside one of the churches. In the meantime Joe had planted himself in the middle of a cluster of local Fianna Fáil activists to try and liven things up. Suddenly he bellowed out as if he were back in Croke Park again. 'Good man, Eugene. Give 'em hell.'

'Give 'em hell,' said one of the Fianna Fáil men standing beside Joe. 'We didn't get hell inside the church this morning and, with all due respects to your friend, the Lord Mayor, I don't think anyone is going to get hell out here either. Finish the meeting and see what you can do in Mellifont, while the monks are meditating.'

The Turnip

Although always a likely target for some sort of physical attack, James Dillon took no special precautions for himself or his platform when addressing fair day and other rallies. The missile thrown in Carrickmacross with enough accuracy to glance off the side of the lorry was a turnip.

'Give that man back his head,' said James, and continued with his speech.

Liam Burke

At the funeral of Liam Burke in August 2005, Fine Gael leader Enda Kenny captured the man very well when he described the former Dáil deputy, senator and Lord Mayor of Cork, as a political colossus in his Cork territory for four decades, who often did things with a bit of humour and devilment. Figuring out which mode Liam was in could sometimes be difficult for those of us outside Cork.

Liam Burke was amongst the best-known personalities within the Fine Gael organisation because of his long service, his affable manner and his famous by-election campaign and victory in Cork North-Central in 1979. It was this by-election win, along with the by-election victory of his Fine Gael colleague Myra Barry in the neighbouring constituency of Cork East on the same day, that focused Garret FitzGerald's Fine Gael on the real possibility of a change of government at the next election.

Because of his knowledge of the Munster area and his friendship with Fine Gael public representatives, Liam was a great man to have guiding a Fine Gael candidate on the 'Senate trail'. The electorate for a Fine Gael Senate candidate is essentially the party's TDs, outgoing senators and county councillors. It is by now the practice to canvass every one of them personally, at home or on their own home ground, at least in the hope of some kind of 'stroke' along the line. The Senate election has a complicated count, and is also a complicated electorate, where no one will give a candidate a total refusal, and where a candidate can often emerge from a canvassing session with far less certainty about the voter's intentions than he had before he arrived.

Burkie knew the electorate and, equally importantly in those pre-mobile-phone days, knew where to get them at any special time of the day or night. This could save days. Liam was also a very good reader of the signals sent out by those being canvassed. On one election, it was noticed that he was taking a particular interest in the progress of a candidate he was showing around. He was not just introducing him to the Senate voters but actively pushing his cause. No one could figure it out because it didn't seem to be of any great advantage to himself. The last call he had to make with this particular candidate was to a councillor living outside the Cork area, but a good friend of Burkie.

The councillor, in addition to his political activities, was a progressive farmer and was milking the cows when the two men called. The councillor continued with his milking while Liam began his pitch. He had no doubt that the candidate he had with him was the man for the number one; he was a man of great promise, and likely to win an extra seat for Fine Gael at the next election; this was obviously the man to be voted into the Senate.

The councillor explained that he would do his best, but that he had some commitments, although nothing definite so far. Anyone would have to be impressed with the sincere endorsements that Liam Burke had given him. Sorry about the milking and that he wasn't able to bring them up to the house for a cup of tea. He wished the would-be senator good luck anyhow in the election.

As Deputy Burke and his companion were leaving through the farm gate, the councillor flagged them down.

'Be careful on the roads,' he said. 'But one thing before you go, Burkie. Will you tell me this? Who will you be giving the number one to yourself?'

Throttle

A Fianna Fáil Minister who was introducing a new piece of legislation was talking at great length, saying nothing substantial, a snow job, just the kind of thing to bring an intervention from Deputy Frank Cluskey (Labour, Dublin South-Central).

'The Minister's foot is full down on the throttle,' he said to him across the House, 'but his brain is in neutral!'

Red Stars over Connemara

(As told by Frank Cluskey's friend Senator Jack Harte)

During the course of the 1981 election Frank Cluskey, leader of the Labour Party and Tánaiste designate, was a candidate in the new constituency of Dublin South-Central, but it was widely predicted that his seat was under pressure from Deputy John O'Connell, who was running as an Independent. And that's the way things turned out. After Cluskey lost his seat, the leadership of Labour and the position of Tánaiste went to Deputy Michael O'Leary.

During the course of the election, Frank committed himself to travel to the important constituencies for Labour. I did not think it was a good idea, especially in view of the manner that John O'Connell was hacking away at his vote. Cluskey insisted that he would stick to the commitment he had made. As his driver, I got him around.

The situation looked very promising for Michael D. Higgins in the new four-seater of Galway West. This would be a major advance for the Labour Party, and everyone from the leader down was giving it full attention.

After a stop for coffee and a smoke in Kinnegad, we were all geared up for the assault on the West. It was a day packed with appointments, delegations and interviews with the local papers, local radio and television. Then followed the ritual visits to convents and even after-Mass speeches. All this was done in torrential rain. To cap everything, the Stickies joined in, harassing Frank while I, as the driver, could have a break, a rest and a sandwich. Frank just stuck to the task without a break or food.

Coming close to 10 pm, Michael D. asked Frank to come to his election headquarters and rally the troops even further — if that were possible — for the election in a few days time. With supporters packed into every corner, Frank was first in the order of speakers and got a rousing reception. After finishing, he pushed his way through the crowd and stood beside me at the back of the room. By this time Michael D. was in full flight, firing on all cylinders, at his very best. It was an emotional occasion for him, realising what capturing the West Galway seat would do for the movement and how it would vindicate the confidence he always had that the breakthrough would come.

Frank Cluskey whispered to me: 'Look at the f——! Here I am drowned to the skin, no food since 10 am and John O'Connell hacking away at my seat in Dublin, and Michael D. ... he's ready to levitate! I hope he'll enjoy the red stars he'll no doubt see in the clear sky over Connemara.'

Michael D. treated us both to a very nice meal at our hotel sometime around midnight.

On our way back from Galway, Frank understandably fell asleep for a while. On awakening, I told him that we were near Athlone. Soon fully alert, he lit up one of his untipped cigars, took a few drags and made the following observation, which I think I have accurately: 'Jack, in about two months time you will be having your lunch in the Members' restaurant. Out of the blue someone will approach you and tell you that he had just come from a visit to Grangegorman where he ran across a fellow with a beard and glasses, who was in a straitjacket. He thinks he is the Tánaiste!'

Bridget Hogan-O'Higgins

'As sure as you're a Fine Gaeler and that's sure enough,' Andy said to James, 'the car that has just swung in there is Bridget's getting home from the Dáil. Whatever they say about it, TDS have to work some terrible hours. Do you think it's too late for us to call?'

This was long before the mobile phone and in most cases before the phone itself. The two got off their bikes to consider the situation.

They were in Kilrickle in south Galway. The Bridget they were talking about was the very popular Dáil deputy Mrs Bridget Hogan-O'Higgins They had both been to her clinic a couple of weeks earlier, seeking her assistance with some little problems. She had a great reputation as a constituency worker.

'She just might have some news with her from Dublin,' James said. 'But it mightn't be right to call at her house at such a late hour, although we both know there would be the height of welcome for us from Bridget, and it would be very handy now that we find ourselves here, instead of having to tidy ourselves up again tomorrow.'

Andy was also beginning to look at it from another side.

'Who knows it might even turn out to be also handier for the deputy! I notice there are lots of lights on in the house.'

The decision in the end was to call. They would be able to check for news but they wouldn't go past the front door, however strongly they were pressed.

Maybe it was because of the lateness of the hour that they weren't as sharp as usual, and even as they walked to the house, they didn't notice that the car outside was not that of the deputy but that of a doctor from the area. He had come to deliver another baby for the large family of Bridget and Michael O'Higgins. For the constituents, it was too late to turn back. They had come level with the door and on they had to go.

Andy and James and the baby arrived at just about the same time. It was congratulations and good wishes all round because, under the circumstances, the unexpected constituents were prevailed on to call in for a few moments.

'Well', said Andy to James as they were heading away, 'it

wasn't the news we came for, but mighty news all the same to be going home with, and a good omen as well.'

'As sure as I'm a Fine Gaeler,' said James as he threw his leg across the saddle and swept out the gate, trying to make up a little bit of the lost time. 'As sure as I'm a Fine Gaeler!'

Honorary Membership

Fianna Fáil was carrying out a national recruiting drive for Ógra Fianna Fáil. One of the meetings was in St Patrick's College, Maynooth, County Kildare, referred to by one student in his preliminary speech as 'the one-time seat of government!' This was a recruitment drive for Fianna Fáil, so that matter was not pursued. The facilities and the location were excellent and they would be needed again. The line-up of speakers were the three local Fianna Fáil deputies. Because it was on his actual territory, Deputy Terry Boylan, a garage owner from Naas and representative of the Kildare constituency in the Dáil, was chairman for the night, and with him were Brian Lenihan and Liam Lawlor, the Fianna Fáil deputies in neighbouring Dublin West.

After the formal meeting had concluded, anyone who wanted to get further information about the party or had an interest in joining was very welcome to stay on. Overall, it was regarded by the representatives from headquarters as a successful meeting both as regards the turnout and the potential for new members, after making due allowances for the fact that it was cold outside and the lecture theatre where the meeting took place had a deserved reputation for the quality of its heating. It was also a good opportunity for the elected representatives to meet their constituents. The final question asked was about the position of non-Irish students — could they join the Fianna Fáil party?

The chairman, Terry Boylan, said that he had just the right man to answer that question, a man who had served as Minister for Foreign Affairs and had represented his country on the

Security Council of the United Nations. Brian at this stage was having an aside meeting with some branch members from Lucan.

Chairman: 'The question being asked, Deputy Lenihan, is on the eligibility of non-Irish students for membership of Fianna Fáil. You'll take that one.'

Back came the reply from Brian without a moment's hesitation: 'Honorary membership … honorary membership.'

8. Elections and All that Jazz

Percy Dockrell

Henry Percy Dockrell was Fine Gael Dáil deputy for Dún Laoghaire from 1951 to 1957 and from 1961 to 1981. He was a very respected, charming man who always did his best for his constituency, but he was not the type of public representative who would go out beating the bushes day and night seeking to whip up work for his constituency clinics, or the kind of man you would see carrying a poster on a protest parade.

Percy would be the first to admit that he was not a great man to attract votes, unlike his constituency colleague Liam Cosgrave, who was constantly among the leading vote-getters in the country. As Percy again would be the first to acknowledge, the transfers from Liam Cosgrave were a great help to him in getting elected.

On the day of the count, Percy was equally laid back, not the type who rushed in for the opening of the boxes. His practice was to arrive in the late evening, by which time a fairly clear pattern would be emerging. He followed the same routine in the 1977 general election. On the steps of Dún Laoghaire Town

Hall where inside the count was proceeding, he met Jim Gill, one of the great Fine Gael workers in the constituency. Jim had copies of the tally sheets with him and told Percy what they contained.

'As you know, Percy, they're still counting. There's a long way to go yet, but I'm afraid you're in trouble; looks like big trouble. We've examined the tally sheets and all our people are saying that your seat is about gone. I'm sorry, but that's being straight about it.'

'Tell me, please, what on earth went wrong, Jim?' Percy asked. 'Did Liam not get enough of a surplus?'

Cluskey on Suicide

Although the leader of the Labour Party and Tánaiste designate in the event of a change of government, Frank Cluskey lost his own Dáil seat in Dublin South-Central in the 1981 general election. While waiting around in the count centre for the usual speeches thanking the returning officer, a young trainee journalist asked him what he was going to do now. Frank's immediate response was — 'Suicide, son.' The trainee reporter, who had no great knowledge of the political scene or of the politicians, was dumbfounded. Frank noticed this and tapped him on the shoulder and reassured him by saying: 'It's not time to worry yet. I haven't decided on the method.'

The Book

Frank Cluskey understood the situation but he wasn't in a very receptive mood when one candidate complained about another candidate on the eve of the election.

'You may very well have a point,' he said, 'but are you aware that the man who made the complaint to you wrote the book on corruption?'

Basil Chubb and David Thornley

Dr Basil Chubb was Professor of Political Science at Trinity College, Dublin, from 1960 to 1991. His book *The Government and Politics of Ireland* was a standard textbook in Irish universities from 1970. Apart from his serious political studies, he became fascinated, long before Frank Hall and *Ballymagash*, with the more off-beat aspects of the work and words of county councillors and he kept in touch with these through regular reading of the regional papers.

In the 1960s Dr David Thornley was an associate professor in Basil Chubb's department. A much younger man than Chubb, he was a popular presenter/commentator on the RTÉ current affairs programme *7 Days*, with a sort of fan base not usually associated with a current affairs programme.

In 1969, to the surprise even of many close colleagues, Thornley contested the general election as a Labour candidate in Dublin North-West. He won the highest number of votes ever achieved in a general election by a Labour candidate in the greater Dublin area. David Thornley later served as a member of the European Parliament.

In 1968 the Fianna Fáil government moved for the second time to replace the use of proportional representation in multi-seat constituencies with the straight vote in single-seat constituencies. I could never fathom why they proposed this since they already had a virtual monopoly of power. Chubb and Thornley together did a major study on the likely outcome of an election under the proposed new system. (I myself made some small contributions to the study, dealing with constituencies where the Trinity matrix might not be suited to the exceptional circumstances prevailing.) The forecast was for Fianna Fáil to win 97 seats in a 147-seat Dáil. It was the subject of a *7 Days* programme and the moment it hit the airwaves the motion to amend the Constitution and jettison the PR system was dead. (That didn't please the yes-vote Director of Elections, Charles J. Haughey, Minister for Agriculture. The next morning when we arrived at the RTÉ offices in Montrose, there was a message for the programme editor, Muiris MacConghail, and myself that Mr Haughey wanted to see us in his office immediately.

'What am I going to do with you boys?' was his opening line.

Despite this, it turned out to be an amicable and restrained meeting, mainly about the findings of the study.

The Chubb/Thornley study became a major focus of discussion and of controversy. For Chubb, with his relaxed manner, it was just another interesting, and he hoped, valuable piece of work. But Thornley, a mercurial man, loved it all. Every morning in an office he shared with Chubb — near the archway entrance to Trinity College and looking out over the Edmund Burke statue — he would give Chubb the latest reaction from their academic friends, in the letters to the newspapers, and among people he met on the street. In these discussions it was Thornley's invariable custom to refer to *our survey*, or *our figures*, or *our exercise* and finally the most favoured of them all, *our prognostication*.

But gradually the Fianna Fáil machine was getting moving. Some of the big guns were limbering up, such as Micheál Ó Móráin, the minister from Castlebar. He had a totally different style to Thornley, but he was a great street fighter. The Trinity pinkos were the targets. As always, the well-drilled Fianna Fáil party members got involved. The Chubb/Thornley forecast was being challenged on all sides. Minds were being changed, and Thornley was feeling the heat.

On one particular morning at the Stephen's Green end of Grafton Street, the journalist Michael Hand told Thornley that the forecast was rubbish. Thornley knew Hand fairly well. What he didn't know was that Michael Hand had an identical twin brother, Jim, so he was taken aback when the second Hand stopped him at the bottom of Grafton Street, only to express the same opinion that the forecast was rubbish in much more robust language than Michael had used. It did not help Thornley's mood when he got to the office and opened his *Irish*

Times to find that the main letter, yet again, was about the Chubb/Thornley forecast.

'I see', he said to Chubb, 'there's another letter in *The Irish Times* criticising your f—— figures, Basil.'

Skulduggery

Politicians are very good at anticipating difficulties that might block their progress even, at times, where no such difficulties exist. All the more surprising then that in their own area of special interest, the proposed switch from manual to electronic voting in the early 2000s, few spotted the danger signals. On the general issue, there were strong arguments to be made on the side of change with instant results or stick with what you have and be sure of getting results sometime. In the final analysis this was about the PR system, maybe not as directly on this occasion as when efforts to change to the straight vote were defeated in two referenda.

The Irish voters love their PR (defects and all) ever since it was introduced on a trial basis in the Borough of Sligo in 1917. Changing anything about it, in the registering of the votes or the delivery of the results, is 'don't touch' territory. In the debate that followed, such as it was, the politicians didn't seem to get involved. It was dominated by the technology experts. They feared that the new voting system or the machines could be interfered with or rigged, or that the secrecy code could be broken. This led to a major review of the programme.

But not everyone was impressed. 'I don't know why these laptop people are so worried,' was the reaction of a rather cynical retired TD. 'Have they any idea of the election skulduggery that can be done with a pencil?'

'Vote early and often' was a slogan taken very seriously in many constituencies at the old Stormont elections in Northern Ireland. And if the many stories are to be believed, some Dáil

Éireann constituencies had their own share of mobile voters travelling between polling booths, and not entirely in the interests of democracy. The practice, I believe, is now much less prevalent.

In addition to the 'mobile votes', there were many other methods of 'stuffing' a ballot box, like the operation that was run in at least one polling station in a West of Ireland constituency. It was greatly facilitated by the fact that the only candidates on the ballot paper were from the two dominant parties, Fianna Fáil and Fine Gael. Furthermore, a part of the constituency was separated, by natural geographical features, from the rest and this part, by good luck or by good vote management, had two outgoing TDs, one Fianna Fáil, one Fine Gael. The deputies were good friends and were often seen having a few drinks together after viciously attacking each other from their respective platforms. They may have had different policies, but they were driven by the same objective — to hold on to their own Dáil seats and let the rest of the country look after itself.

What about the hints of promotion they had got from their respective headquarters if they delivered the extra seat? What use was a promise of promotion if you didn't get elected yourself in the first place? No seat, no Mercedes stareen anyway.

The presiding officer in the particular polling station and the polling clerk had strong political connections, one on one side and one on the other. Maybe that's how they had got the jobs in the first place. As the day wore on and the votes were cast, the only other people around the place were the personating officers, again by the nature of the job on this occasion, one Fianna Fáil and one Fine Gael. During the day the polling clerk had ensured a very thorough job of marking up the electoral register. With about half an hour to go to the close of voting, he did another check. There were thirty-one unused voting papers. He and all others present knew exactly who those thirty-one were, knew them personally. Most of them were in England, or in America, or even over in the graveyard.

Polling Clerk: I don't think there'll be anyone else coming to vote. That looks like it for the day.

Presiding Officer: The radio is saying there's going to be a big turnout all over the country. I have a sinking feeling both our men, John and James [the local deputies — not their real names], could be in trouble. That would be a terror.

Polling Clerk: The changes in the constituency boundaries could do a lot of damage to them both.

Presiding Officer: We wouldn't like to have to go with our problems to someone living thirty miles away. Who knows what kind of reception we might get. Distance never helps influence. People don't realise the power of their votes … but that little lot of unused votes could save the seat of one of our TDs.

Polling Clerk: If they were divided up half and half, one for one, they might even save the two seats for the area.

The strategy was agreed (as obviously previously arranged) by a nod and a wink, with never a word spoken. Some of these fellows could send a text with their eyebrows.

Presiding Officer: What about the number twos?

Polling Clerk: I don't think we should do anything about the number twos. That would be interfering. Anyway, if things work out the way I see it, they'll never come into play.

They had got down to the last few votes in the split-up when the Presiding Officer was passed a message.

Presiding Officer: I believe there's one man down in the pub who might still stray up to vote. We had better hold back an unmarked voting paper.

Polling Clerk: I don't think he'd ever make it up against the hill at this time of the day, but I agree we should hold back the vote in case and then a few more with it. In the circumstances it might be better not to draw too much attention to the size of our turnout. We are not looking to win any medals for that.

On the stroke of nine the last vote was marked up. It was the vote of a local woman who had died fairly recently. It was due to go to John. 'Fair enough,' said James's personating officer. 'Sure it's the way she'd have voted anyhow herself if she were in a position to do so.'

9. Devotion

Oliver's Piety
— Michael Finlan

Oliver J. Flanagan, noted for his piety, was among the army of TDS and Senators sent into Mayo on the campaign trail. Around noon one day, Oliver J. sat down to a meal in the dining room of his hotel. He had barely begun to eat when the peals of a nearby church bell were carried into the dining room — the Angelus. Immediately Oliver J. downed his knife and fork, got to his feet, bowed his head, crossed himself and began reciting the prayers of the Angelus — aloud! Confronted with such a display of piety, the other guests in the dining room had to stand up too and join in the prayers.

[Related by Michael Finlan, Western correspondent of *The Irish Times*, in a piece written for Donal Foley's column 'Man Bites Dog' during a by-election campaign in Mayo West in November 1975. The by-election was caused by the death of Henry Kenny, Parliamentary Secretary to the Minister for Finance 1969–75 and Fine Gael Dáil deputy for Mayo South

1954–69 and Mayo West 1969–75. It was won by his son, Enda
Kenny. After appearing in *The Irish Times*, the 'Prayers with
Meals' piece was picked up by several publications, including
The Spectator in London.]

Confessions

Alderman Seán McManus, Fianna Fáil Mayor of Sligo, had a
very busy Christmas Eve, with several functions to attend and
several official visits to make.

In addition to being mayor, he was also a social welfare
officer, a job that he carried out with great care and consideration. Again his help was in much demand at
Christmastime.

Despite all these obligations, the Mayor managed somehow
to get to the cathedral in time for his own confession in the days
when confessions still had queues. The size of the queue and the
nameplate on the box usually generated some good-natured
jockeying for position.

Someone, understanding the busy schedule he had, gave way
in the queue to speed things up for the mayor. As he came out,
Mayor McManus held the door of the confessional box open for
the next in line. 'For God's sake will you shut that door,' came
an all too familiar voice from the shadows behind the
confessional box. 'Can't you see the state I'm in? It's you I'm
looking for, not the confessor.'

Jim and the Pope

Occupants of an Irish tourist coach viewing the sights around
St Peter's in Rome were quick to spot the Lord Mayor of Dublin,
Jim Mitchell, and his wife, Patsy, who were later that day to be
received in private audience by Pope Paul vi.

'Yez are a lovely couple,' one of the tourists tried shouting
over the noise. 'A credit to the city,' said another. Soon the full

chorus was going and the inevitable flags, wherever they are kept, began to appear. The Mayor had no objection to the attention even if it was in Rome and not in Dublin West. This was a day free from politics but inevitably there would be some positive fall-out. 'Keep it going' seemed to be the attitude of the Lord Mayor as further Irish, including a sprinkling of nuns and priests, were attracted by the flags.

When Jim Mitchell started his year as Lord Mayor in 1976, he was, at twenty-nine years, the youngest holder of that position in its eight-hundred-year history. In 1977 he was elected Fine Gael Dáil deputy for Dublin West and, in an area that was never easy for his party, he built up a powerful machine and vote-getting organisation.

He was also a man with a great sense of humour, who liked nothing better than 'winding up' his friends in politics and in Patsy's native Loughrea where he went on summer holidays, and where some mightn't have expected this kind of approach from a Lord Mayor of Dublin and a cabinet minister in Garret FitzGerald's government.

He candidly admitted that he enjoyed the trappings of office as Lord Mayor, like moving with Patsy and the family into the Mansion House, being driven around the city by chauffeur, and responding to the invitations, as he now was, to a private audience with the Pope.

The Irish Ambassador to the Holy See was in charge of protocol. Although they did have a brief rehearsal, the whole thing was extremely simple.

The absolute and golden rule was that the person being received in private audience did not speak in any circumstances until the Pope had first spoken. Then the words to be used were: 'It's a great honour to meet your Holiness.'

Afterwards every one of the Irish grouping wanted to know just one thing.

'How did it go, Lord Mayor?' or 'How did it go, Jimmy?' They all wanted to know fast.

The Lord Mayor, after what he considered to be a suitable pause, responded: 'The Pope stole my opening line!'

Haughey after Mass
— Michael Finlan

Charlie Haughey was up in Donegal, busy canvassing in a by-election. Surrounded by a crowd of Fianna Fáil myrmidons, he arrived outside a chapel gate one Sunday morning and mounted a platform, which had been set up there in good time to catch the congregation coming out from eleven o'clock Mass.

Haughey was well launched into a spirited speech when suddenly the church bell just inside the gate began ringing. The Angelus was announcing time for prayer, not politics. Without missing a beat, Haughey paused for a split second, then modified his fiery political oratory into the reverential tone of a devout monk at prayer and led the assembled politicos and punters in reciting the Angelus — word perfect, it might be added. As soon as he brought the prayers to a close, he paused again for a second, then instantly shed his air of sanctity and turned into a political demon again, calling down curses on Fine Gael, Labour and the rest of his opponents.

[Related by Michael Finlan, Western correspondent for *The Irish Times* in his by-election notebook in November 1980. The Dáil vacancy was caused by the death of the Ceann Comhairle, Joe Brennan (Fianna Fáil), former minister and Dáil deputy in Donegal 1951–80. The by-election was won by Clem Coughlan, who later died in a car accident.]

The Slow-moving Statues

The year was 1995. The weather was lousy. Statues were moving everywhere in the country. Where the statues weren't moving, the Blessed Virgin was appearing. The most beleaguered man in the country was the Minister for Agriculture, Austin Deasy. The farmers were in near revolt. The rain was incessant and there would be no feed for the cattle that winter.

Still, fair play to Austin Deasy, he travelled around the country, even though he knew the reception was bound to be hostile. He came to my own constituency of Sligo–Leitrim. We didn't have any moving statue, but we had a visit from the Blessed Virgin in Carns in west Sligo. There was an estimated 20,000 people there one August Sunday, including my good friend and colleague Deputy Matt Brennan (Fianna Fáil, Sligo–Leitrim), who believes he saw something.

There was a meeting of the cabinet, probably a special meeting to deal with the farmers' situation. The story goes that it was late in starting because the Minister for Agriculture had been delayed. When he arrived, he apologised, saying that he had been held up in the traffic.

'What was the traffic problem, Austin?' another Minister, and not Austin's best friend, asked, interested in getting away fast.

'Ah ... it was the moving statues. They were in front of me all the way and wouldn't let me through!' Austin replied.

———

Of course, there is another form of devotion for which Irish politicians are famous, namely a passion for sport.

John Wilson

It was the day of the Oireachtas Golf Outing at Oliver Barry's fine course in north County Dublin. It was known as the Joe Brennan Memorial Cup (Joe was a very popular deputy with people on all sides of the House and the naming of the Cup reflects that). As always at these gatherings, the speeches were good, mainly concentrating on the doings or misdoings of Dáil deputies and senators past and present, most of them apocryphal yarns.

After listening to a few of these anecdotes, an unknown 'guest', who had strayed into the wrong function but had recognised some of the TDs, asked if John Wilson was there or any of the Cavan people. He had a story himself he would like to tell. As it turned out, none of the Cavan public representatives was present, but the visitor was given every encouragement, including a pint put in front of him by Deputy Paul McGrath, to tell the story anyhow. It was that kind of session.

There was this man (we'll call him Seamus McDyer for convenience) living in Glangevlen in County Cavan. A small farmer with three great loves in his life — Fine Gael politics, Gaelic football, and drink, more or less in that order, but it has to be said that his drinking was frequently curtailed because of cash flow problems. All he had was the farmer's dole plus the sale of the odd Aberdeen Angus bullock at the fair, and you had to fight a hard bargain with the jobbers for every few bob that you got. So it was Saturday night and Sunday night in the pub, and on the dry for the rest of the week.

Seamus knew everything about Cavan football. Just nominate the year you wanted to know about and he was away. Along with the names of the players, he always had a little cv on their achievements and finished with his own assessment of their abilities. His favourite team, of course, was the 1947 team that won the All-Ireland Final played at the Polo Grounds in New York. A favourite player was Big Tom O'Reilly, who later became an Independent Dáil deputy himself, although he could stick Leinster House for no longer than one Dáil term. As he departed, he said that, despite a guaranteed safe 'football seat' for the rest of his life, he would rather make a living going around collecting empty bottles than doing the work of a TD. Another favourite of Seamus McDyer was Commmandant John Joe O'Reilly at centre-half back, but the darling of them all, as far as Seamus was concerned, was the right-half back, John Wilson. His cv always ended with the words 'a classical footballer'. Why Seamus chose this description is not known, but it is thought that it may have derived in some way from the fact that Seamus knew of Mr Wilson's ability as a classical scholar.

When it was announced, out of the blue, that the Dublin-based John Wilson, the footballer, would be a candidate for Fianna Fáil in Cavan at the next general election, the lads couldn't wait for the Saturday night in the pub to hear the reaction of Seamus, the Fine Gael man, to his favourite player going to tog out for the other side.

Came the night and Seamus was there in his usual corner. The pints were being lined up in front of him. Gradually his cronies levered the conversation around to Gaelic football. Someone asked him about the Polo Grounds and the Cavan team on that day. He went through it more or less as usual, but this time made no mention of the right-half back, John Wilson. Nice try but there was no way the crowded pub was going to let Seamus give them the slip. Too much had been invested in the exercise.

'What about Wilson?' came the inevitable supplementary. 'Was he any good on the day at all?'

Seamus pondered for a while as if he had never applied his mind to the question before.

'Well,' he said, 'he'd be the "wake" link, wouldn't he?
He'd be the "wake" link.'

Jack Lynch in Studio

The story is told that, when it came to politics, Jack Lynch
finally decided between Fianna Fáil and Fine Gael, both suitors,
with the toss of a coin. It's unlikely now that we'll ever know if
this really happened. The reality is that Jack Lynch didn't need
either party to get to Leinster House, but was quickly on the
ladder to the top through the political party he had chosen.

There was no doubt of his steely determination on the
playing pitches. You don't collect seven All-Ireland medals for
just walking around Croke Park after the Artane Boys' Band.

Des Fisher likes to tell the story of his coolness later as a
politician in testing times. It was the night of the 'We won't
stand idly by' speech in 1969, broadcast from the RTÉ Studios in
Montrose. When the Taoiseach arrived he was met, as always, by
the senior person there — on that night, Des Fisher himself, the
Deputy Head of RTÉ News. Des, a man of vast experience in
television, radio and newspapers, immediately noticed the
condition of the Taoiseach's script. To begin with, it was typed
in single space, as distinct from the double space invariably used
throughout the media (when working for the *Irish Press* I saw
triple space being used in the typing of de Valera's speeches,
leaving the extra space in for the inevitable changes, as Dev
weighed each word). Already there had been corrections and
deletions on parts of the Taoiseach's speech. After consultations
with his people, Jack agreed that it would be a good idea to have
it retyped. And this was done after the confidentiality matters
were sorted out.

After that, the Taoiseach rang his wife, Máirín, in their
Garville Avenue home in Dublin. Des then invited him to come
round to the hospitality room afterwards (unless he was under

enormous pressure, Jack always called to the hospitality room after broadcasts for his trademark Paddy whiskey) and then Des wished him good luck with the broadcast. Before he left to do his broadcast, the Taoiseach asked Des if he could oblige him by checking to see — if the Sports Department was still open — how Glen Rovers had fared.

This was something that even Des Fisher, the complete professional, hadn't anticipated. Furthermore, all sports were a blank to him. The easiest way to put it was that he had never heard of Glen Rovers or that he had been living for a year in Wimbledon before it struck him that this was where they played the tennis. Anyhow he was able to answer the query for his guest before the latter went on air, but now cannot recollect whether it was good news or bad news.

Give Garret a Hurley

(As told by Louis J. Belton)

Taoiseach Garret FitzGerald was attending the All Ireland Hurling Final in Croke Park, Dublin, as all Taoisigh do. Now we know he wasn't a fan or mad about hurling, but he went along because he was Taoiseach, and he was in the Hogan Stand. As it happens, this was in the pre-helmet days. (Now all players have to wear helmets and there has been a remarkable improvement in the quality of the gear both for its primary job of protecting the player and also in comfort for the wearers. In those days you only saw the odd helmet.) In this Final there were a few very bad clashes. Two or three of the players were injured and they had white bandages on their heads, and the blood was coming through. The pitch was starting to look like a war zone.

As soon as the match was over, Garret zoomed down off the Hogan Stand. His car was underneath, engine purring, waiting to collect him. But a few journalists spotted him and took off after him, not an easy job any day of the week, but especially in those times when Garret was in full flow. But they did catch him just as he was getting into the car. (By the way, he told this story himself.)

One of them said to the Taoiseach: 'How did you enjoy the game?'

'Oh,' he said, 'very good game, very good, very tense, very close.' The other guy got in with his question.

'Garret, did you ever play hurling yourself?'

'No,' he said, 'I didn't. I played a small bit of cricket, but I never played hurling.'

Garret wasn't away from the journalists yet. As he was closing the door, the other journalist came back with his last shot.

'Garret,' he said, 'how would you like to have been out there today on the pitch with a hurley in your hand?'

Garret paused, looked at him and said, 'I wouldn't like to have been out there *without* a hurley in my hand!'

Dick Spring

Dick Spring seemed the perfect choice as guest of honour at the awards presentation to the Sports Stars of the Year in Jurys Hotel in Ballsbridge, Dublin. He was leader of the Labour Party, Tánaiste and a cabinet minister, and an excellent speaker in the Dáil or after dinner. Dick was a formidable and versatile sportsman himself — in rugby where he was capped for Ireland three times, in Gaelic football and hurling where he played for Kerry, and he could always be relied on to bring in a good golf score in Ballybunion, even with the distraction of President Bill Clinton in the same group.

Still, when he completed the presentations and got to the rostrum, he told us, the guests, that he hadn't felt fully comfortable in his role. With the best athletes in the country in the audience, he asked himself why he should be centre stage: 'Then I saw some of my rugby friends in the distance. There was

Moss Keane with 51 caps for Ireland. There was Willie John McBride with 63 caps for Ireland. And there was Fergus Slattery with 61 caps.

'So I did a quick calculation. With Moss, Willie John, Fergus and myself, we had 178 caps between us!'

10. The Necessary Business of Death and Dying

Paddy Burke

The newsroom of the *Irish Press*, overlooking the Liffey at Burgh Quay, was generally a noisy place in the 1950s, with three or four news editors, ten or more reporters around at any given time, and farther down, the sub-editors, all in open-plan offices. For one short period around midday, things would go a little quieter with the change in shifts and with the first edition of the *Evening Press* already on its way to the streets. Then one particular phone extension in a corner of the newsroom would ring. Everyone knew who the caller would be.

'This is Deputy Paddy Burke. To whom have I the pleasure of speaking?' The Mayo-born deputy had a regular morning routine before heading off for Leinster House. If there was a funeral or two funerals in his North Dublin constituency, he would attend. Immediately afterwards he would head for the nearest public phone box (he could write a directory on them) to make that call to the *Irish Press*. The message was always the same.

At that time the *Irish Press* was devoting considerable editorial space to reports of funerals, particularly of old IRA veterans. If the newspaper was reporting on a funeral he had attended, Paddy wanted to ensure that he was listed as 'amongst the attendance'. So the stories of Deputy Burke and funeral-going grew until he became the central character of what has been, down the years, the most frequently told political anecdote of them all.

The Dublin North constituency was then a three-seat constituency and to a considerable extent still a farming area. The other Dáil deputies were Éamonn Rooney (Fine Gael) and Seán Dunne (Labour). These men didn't have the time, the stamina or the desire to match the morning routine of their Fianna Fáil colleague. However, at this particular funeral they both turned up, where, to their great surprise, there was no sign of Deputy Burke, and this was 'an important funeral'. They looked around for him, but no Paddy.

'The poor man must be seriously ill,' Deputy Rooney said in mock sympathy.

The funeral procession was coming in their direction. Deputy Dunne, a very tall man, could now get a different view.

'I don't want to be the person to bring you bad news at a funeral,' Deputy Dunne whispered to Deputy Rooney, 'but he's here.'

'I couldn't have missed him,' said Rooney.

'Well, you did, and so did I, because we were searching for him in the wrong places. Take a closer look at the front of the procession. The man we thought was the new priest!'

There he was … Dáil Deputy Paddy Burke, wearing a black soutane, a white surplice trimmed with Carrickmacross lace, newly starched it seemed. He was carrying the cross, leading the procession at the same kind of dignified pace as the bishop on St Patrick's Day. There was a very un-bishoplike wink as he drew level with his Dáil colleagues, then a quick return to the bow and the nod. As the procession went past, a local mourner tugged at Seán Dunne's overcoat.

'Do you see that man gone up there carrying the cross? That's our local Dáil Deputy Paddy Burke. He goes to every funeral. Isn't he a great man?'

Seán Dunne, who occasionally dropped a few Latin tags into his conversation, made some reply. At a distance, it didn't sound like *Deo Gratias*.

That's Loyalty for You

(As told by Louis J. Belton)

You could hardly get a more Fine Gael family than the Reynolds of Ballinamore, County Leitrim. Pat Joe was a Dáil deputy, as were his father and mother before him and his son, Gerard, after him. Well, anyway, Pat Joe got a call to attend to this well-known Fianna Fáil supporter who unfortunately was feeling that his time was short. And Pat Joe said: 'Of course I'll go out to visit him.' And he did go out and visit him. And the man said out of the bed: 'Pat Joe, thanks for coming. I want you to do me a favour. I want to join Fine Gael.'

Pat Joe was stunned. He said: 'What! Are you sure?'

'Yes, Pat Joe. I want to join Fine Gael.'

'Well', said Pat Joe, 'I haven't a membership card with me, but I have some at home. I'll go and get one.'

So he did and he came back and your man signed up and paid whatever it was to join Fine Gael — a pound or two pounds. He shook hands and left, saying 'God bless.'

The son became inquisitive and said to the father: 'Why did you bring Pat Joe Reynolds out here? Sure you never voted for that crowd in your life.'

And the father said: 'Well to tell you the truth, I'm after joining Fine Gael.'

'You what!'

'I'm after joining Fine Gael.'

'What did you do that for?'

'Well, isn't it better for one of them to go than one of us?'

Martin Corry

There are many stories about the Cork Fianna Fáil stalwart Martin Corry, and the late Jim Gibbons liked to tell the one of the morning Fianna Fáil headquarters in Upper Mount Street rang him (Gibbons) at his Kilkenny home instructing him to proceed forthwith to Cork to represent headquarters at the funeral of a well-known Fianna Fáil deputy.

Gibbons freely admitted that it was highly inconvenient for him on that particular morning and that he proceeded to Cork in bad humour. In torrential rain he arrived late, and trudged a long way through the cemetery until he saw up ahead the sodden mourners, many of them elderly party workers, gathered round the graveside.

Working his way through the crowd, he edged in beside Corry, who was standing with head bare and bowed in the downpour, contemplating the coffin that had just been lowered into the grave. Gibbons suddenly felt ashamed of his earlier irritation at having to attend, and gently pressed Corry's arm, murmuring sympathy.

Without raising his head, Corry mumbled out of the corner of his mouth: 'Move the writ on the twenty-third; we're putting up the bleddy widow!'

Nothing personal, just business.

Telegrams

Leinster House once had its own post office conveniently located at the bottom of the grand staircase. That was the time when members had to buy their own stamps. But in the morning the main post office activity had to do with telegrams. Deputies were getting off their messages of sympathy after reading the death notices in the morning papers. They regarded it as very important that, when the telegram boys set out on their bicycles from the various post offices in the constituencies, *their* message was there along with those of their constituency colleagues, or, even better still, without those of constituency colleagues!

For a period in the late 1960s, Donegal had two cabinet ministers, Neil T. Blaney and Joe Brennan, and also Cormac Breslin as Ceann Comhairle of Dáil Éireann. Unlike back-benchers, each had a private secretary and personal staff. The first duty of the private secretary in the morning was to collect the national papers, circle the death notices relevant because of location or other connections, and have the marked papers on their boss's desk when he arrived. In most ministers' offices, that was a priority and probably still is today (although local radio has diminished the effectiveness of the national papers as a major source of comprehensive information on deaths).

On one particular morning, both Neil Blaney and Cormac Breslin were very surprised to see the death notice of a party stalwart at the top of their special papers. Both had seen the man recently, looking in the whole of his health and talking enthusiastically about a general election. But there it was. Both knew his address very well, since he had been at one time a cumann secretary. We'll call the party stalwart James Murphy for the purpose of the story. So telegrams were dispatched immediately, which meant at roughly the same time, from Neil Blaney and Cormac Breslin. They and all the other office-holders used a standard wording.

Now Joe Brennan had a residence in Delgany, County Wicklow, at the time and on the odd morning liked to play a few holes of golf on the nearby course. This was one of those mornings. So he was late getting in to his office. The routine was the same as with his colleagues. He first read the death notices. Like the others, he was shocked to read of James Murphy's death. He decided to ring his own home in Mountcharles, County Donegal, to see what the story was: there was a James Murphy dead. The deceased was from the same parish as the party stalwart, the same address, but it wasn't *their* James Murphy. No telegram would be needed in this case.

Furthermore, Joe Brennan took the additional precaution of telling his private secretary to ensure that, whatever happened, no telegram got out by accident.

Later in the day Blaney and Breslin discovered their mistakes. Consultations followed and it was decided that this was serious enough for the minister to drive to the constituency at the weekend (in the ministerial Merc) and apologise to James Murphy, for them both, for the mistake.

James understood. 'Sure we got telegrams, letters and Mass cards from people all over the country,' he told Neil. 'I didn't know I was that popular. Maybe I should be a candidate myself at the next election.'

'It's good of you to take it that way', Neil said, 'and I'm here to apologise on behalf of Cormac also. As Ceann Comhairle, Cormac cannot get involved as much as he used to.'

'A decent man, Cormac,' said James. 'Tell him not to worry. But I notice that my good friend Joe Brennan, the lazy f——, didn't send any telegram at all.'

Death Notices
Reading the death notices in the morning papers used to be a first job for politicians. The Ministers had it done for them by their private secretaries, who would read through the notices in all the papers and then mark those from the Minister's constituency, and leave the papers neatly folded for his first read. Nowadays they all listen to the local radio. One politician felt he should put on record his gratitude for the very thorough and dignified manner in which his local radio broadcasts these announcements. Councillors love motions, and surely there was some motion he could put down somewhere to acknowledge the work. There was one thing, however, that worried him and he didn't know what to do about it. On a day when there was no one he knew dead, thank God, after the list had been completed, he was inclined to feel a little bit disappointed.

Oliver J. Flanagan

Oliver J. Flanagan was a great man for funerals. He once told me that as a Dáil deputy he felt he had a certain obligation to attend the funerals of his constituents. Naturally it wasn't possible to go to them all, but because of the relative proximity of Leinster House to his electoral base in Laois–Offaly, he was able to make an appearance at a very large proportion of them. Estimating with any accuracy the total he might have attended is difficult. But Michael Ring of Mayo, who, like Oliver J., represents a five-seat constituency and keeps up a similar pace on funerals, believes that the average would have been maybe ten a week. And Oliver J. was forty-four years a TD. (As a one-time Dáil deputy myself, I believe that the presence of a local deputy at a funeral is greatly appreciated by the relatives and the community.)

Certainly this attendance at funerals did Oliver J. no harm at all at the polling booths. At every general election after he first got into the Dáil in 1943 until he retired, as Father of the House, in 1987, he headed the poll in Laois–Offaly. Some of the legendary great vote-getters in Irish elections, like Daniel O'Connell and Jack Lynch, did not do much better than that, comparatively speaking.

In 1969 the RTÉ current affairs programme *7 Days*, on which I was a political commentator, decided to do a series of film biographies of high-profile backbench deputies. Oliver J. was a natural for inclusion. At our planning meetings we considered how we should cover his attendance at the funerals.

Remember that this was a time when television in general, and the near monopoly channel of RTÉ in particular, was much more sensitive than it is today. Would it be fair to relatives of the deceased to show a politician doing his rounds outside the church or in the graveyard? The decision of the then editor, Muiris MacConghail, was to do the relevant filming anyhow, put it in the can, and we could decide later how to use it. There was no hesitation or doubt as far as Oliver J. himself was concerned. He would be going to a funeral at Emo, County Laois. The night before, he knew that we would be staying at the County Arms Hotel, Birr. We were just beginning dinner when the manageress, Jo Loughnane (who was later to become my wife), told me that Oliver J. was on the phone and wanted to talk to me. I assumed that this was it: that he was finally going to call off the funeral filming at Emo.

'About that funeral tomorrow in Emo …', Oliver J. started. Immediately I assured him that in no way would there be any danger that our filming would intrude on the privacy of the bereaved or on the dignity of the occasion.

'Sure I know that well, Ted,' said Oliver J. 'What I wanted to tell you was that there is a much better funeral in Tullamore the following day.'

––––

Oliver had an elaborate network system of being quickly informed when someone died, apart from the routine check of the morning papers. Usually there was a designated person in each parish or half-parish; sometimes it was the parish priest himself. They used to say in the constituency that he knew about the funerals before the undertakers.

But no system is perfect. On one very important occasion the network failed. The deceased was one of his key men, faithful, hard-working and long-serving, even dating back to the days of Oliver J.'s own party, the Monetary Reform Party. Naturally the deputy was expected to be there at the removal of the remains to the church on the Sunday evening. When he didn't turn up, there was no great panic amongst his supporters. He'd be there for the Mass and the burial on the next day.

But when the Mass started and Oliver J. had not appeared, a few friends at the back of the church got worried. Better put through a phone call, they decided. This was in the days before the mobile, but the priest's housekeeper was only too glad to give them the use of the presbytery phone. The deputy was finally hunted down at a meeting of Laois County Council. He hadn't heard a word about the death of his great friend and supporter.

'Could I still make it?' he asked.

'You just might, Oliver, but you'd want to hurry. I'll see if we can slow things down a little bit here.'

They were lowering the coffin into the grave when Oliver J. finally arrived.

'There's only one person you need worry about,' his friends briefed him as he came into the graveyard. 'That's his son standing over there beside your friend the parish priest. There are no other close relatives.'

What they had no time to tell him and what he didn't know himself was that the father and his son had not got on. The father was a bit awkward, a crusty man, very old-fashioned in his ways. He did not favour his son spending time in the pub, going to dances, attending football matches. Girlfriends were out. Times had sort of passed the young man by. Father and son had not had a normal conversation with each other for maybe ten years.

'Great old friend of mine,' said Oliver as he expressed his sympathies.

'Yes, Oliver.'

'As decent a man as there ever was between here and Slieve Bloom.'

'Yes, Oliver.'

'I could always rely on him to be first man out on polling day.'

'Yes, Oliver.'

After a while Oliver J. was beginning to get the feeling that something was different here. The responses he was getting were too routine, with no real feeling. He decided to try a different approach. He then placed a comforting hand on the bereaved son's shoulder, lowered his voice a little and continued, 'Tell me, my good man, was your father long complaining?'

'All his f—— life, Oliver. All his f—— life.'

Charles J. Haughey's Yacht

Charles J. Haughey had completed his holidays in Innisvickalaun, boarded his boat *The Taurima* in Dingle Harbour and set off for his home base of Howth Harbour. Conditions at sea were good, the only difficulty being a mist somewhat restricting visibility. Five people were aboard. *The Taurima* was due to pass Mizen Head around two in the morning.

Then, without any alert or warning of danger, the yacht crashed into the north side of Mizen. Within twenty minutes it had sunk. All on board had scrambled on to *The Taurima* life raft and the inflatable dinghy.

The Baltimore lifeboat was alerted and the rescue operation completed very efficiently. This was a narrow escape from what could have been a major tragedy. Inevitably, in view of the principal involved, this danger in no way stopped or even inhibited the stories and the anecdotes. They flourished, spreading with great speed from Mizen Head to Malin Head.

One of these is of Mr Haughey in Baltimore that morning thanking all those involved in the rescue operation. Despite his ordeal, he was in sparkling form. He shook hands, spoke to everyone, expressed his thanks and appreciation time and again and promised that if there was anything he could do for the local community or for any individual, he'd be only too pleased to help. They all acknowledged the offer and some clapped. It was a sort of thank you ritual.

Then, much to the surprise of everyone a young man of about six foot two or three, with the physique of a Seán Óg Ó hAilpín, said that he had one request that he would like to put to Mr Haughey, seeing that he had been good enough to make the offer. If Mr Haughey couldn't help, that would be alright.

'There is one thing that I would like, Mr Haughey, and that's a State funeral.'

'Well I'm afraid I can't help you there,' said the Taoiseach, taken aback like everyone else. 'State funerals are for Presidents, ex-Taoisigh, very limited.... Tell me why is a young fellow like you concerning yourself about any sort of funeral anyhow? You should be thinking of playing for Cork in the red jersey in an All Ireland Final. You look the picture of health to me.... There's nothing wrong with you, thank God.'

'No, Mr Haughey, there is nothing wrong with me right now. But there will be very shortly, and seriously wrong with me at that … when I get home and my father finds out that I was one of the people who rescued you!'

The Fine Gael deputy in the area at the time was Paddy Sheehan, the man who famously said on being elected to the Dáil in 1981 that the mismanagement of the economy by Fianna Fáil had meant that there was nothing left in his constituency except briars, bullocks and bachelors. Paddy had lines like that to sprinkle around at will. He was particularly friendly with C.J. Haughey and the two were involved in some hilarious exchanges in the Dáil when Mr Haughey, as Taoiseach, was regularly taking the order of business. Paddy was one of the first on the air to express his thanks to God that a major tragedy had been averted with *The Taurima* and that Mr Haughey and his friends had hardly got their socks wet at the Mizen.

Later when telling the story of *The Taurima*, Paddy, who lives in Goleen, the last village before heading out to the Mizen, had some additional thoughts on the near tragedy.

'God forbid, but can you imagine what the situation would be here if anything did happen to my friend Charlie? His supporters would organise a Commemoration Sunday or maybe a Commemoration Weekend and they'd erect a monument the size of the lighthouse. They'd be here in their thousands. Jaysus, it would be ten times worse than Béal na mBláth.'

11. The Stuff of Legend

Erskine Childers on the Road

For his Presidential Election campaign in 1973, Erskine Childers memorably travelled aboard a bus known as 'The Wanderly Wagon'. Here Seán Duignan, political correspondent, takes us on a journey in the wagon from Belmullet to Sligo, the final stage in a long day's travel:

> With the bevy of journalists along for the ride, the presidential candidate's idiosyncratic ways during the nationwide tour spawned a stream of anecdotes. At one stage when Brian Lenihan urged him to wave to the people en route, he responded: 'But I don't know them, Brian.'
>
> On another occasion, Childers icily informed a photographer who asked him to pose next to a certain western politician: 'I would not be seen dead beside that reptile!'
>
> The result was that a number of the media 'boys on the bus' decided that he was basically unelectable.
>
> They were confirmed in that view on a night of

torrential rain in the proverbial bog below Belmullet in County Mayo. A drenched group of Fianna Fáil supporters had been waiting at a crossroads to cheer on their champion. The local Fianna Fáil Cumann Chairman flagged down the bus and requested that Mr Childers address the assembled troops, to which he replied: 'Sorry, I must go to Sligo!' It was only after the doughty Chairman prevented the bus from proceeding by the simple expedient of physically barring the way that Childers was prevailed upon to address his admirers through a bus window.

'My dear people, I must go to Sligo but you can listen to me tonight after the news on Radio Éireann....'

'Jaysus, keep going,' pleaded one of his Fianna Fáil entourage.

As if suddenly inspired, the candidate obliged, '... but I can say to you: I have seen the wonders of the world, the mighty Pyramids, the Great Wall of China, the incomparable Taj Mahal. I have climbed every mountain and I can tell you this: YOU'RE BETTER OFF AS YOU ARE!'

A ragged cheer rang out from the saturated ranks of the faithful and the bus proceeded to Sligo without further hindrance.

Notwithstanding the accumulated wisdom of the hacks, Erskine Childers also proceeded to be comfortably elected Úachtarán na hÉireann in 1973.

[Seán Duignan, *One Spin on the Merry-Go-Round*, Blackwater Press, 1995]

Bon Appétit

The *Bon Appétit* story, the most repeated political story doing the rounds some years ago, was said to have originated with the

Irish members of the European Parliament in Strasbourg. However, it has all the hallmarks of an old classic that has been reworked and repolished. Anyhow, it's now part of the repertoire of many parliamentarians in the EU member states, with different names and different locations giving it added flavour.

Like all these stories, it has different versions. The best telling — to suit an Irish audience — I heard was at a function in the Sligo Park Hotel, by Tommie Gorman, then European editor of RTÉ based in Brussels (now Northern Ireland editor of RTÉ).

A newly elected Irish member of the European parliament was on his first journey to Strasbourg in that capacity. He was staying in the favoured hotel, generally full at such times with MEPS and parliament-related personnel. We'll call the Irish MEP Máirtín Murray for the purposes of this story. Breakfast at the hotel was self-service and Máirtín had got himself a convenient table near the central supply line. He was suddenly joined by a stranger (as it turned out, a French Gaullist MEP from Brittany).

'Bon appétit,' said Jean the Frenchman as he sat down.

Máirtín was concentrating on the job in hand — a hearty breakfast — and wasn't paying attention to the new arrival. He didn't catch what the Frenchman had said but assumed that he was giving his name by way of introduction. In response, Máirtín simply gave his own name.

'Máirtín Murray.'

That night a number of the Irish MEPS had dinner at a favourite restaurant. When the steaks arrived, someone from the group — probably a long-serving MEP, well versed in the local customs and practices — said 'Bon Appétit'.

This led to Máirtín telling them the details of his experience that morning with the Frenchman at breakfast. Not to worry, they told him, he would probably meet him at breakfast the following morning and they could have a chat. Máirtín Murray decided to be down early, and so he was. But not quite soon enough. Already at the rashers and scrambled eggs stage was the Frenchman. He spotted Máirtín and a few friends arriving. He acknowledged his breakfast companion of the previous morning with a wave in his direction and then wished him and all his friends 'Máirtín Murray'.

Thundering Disgrace

As revealed in the Government papers released in December 2006, it fell to my lot to inform the Taoiseach, Liam Cosgrave, of developments at Columb Barracks, Mullingar, on the day of the 'Thundering Disgrace' remark.

The Taoiseach's note of his involvement in the affair begins: 'On Monday, 18 October, I was informed by the Head of the Government Information Services (Ted Nealon), and sub-sequently by the Minister for Justice (Patrick Cooney), that the Minister for Defence had departed from his script at Columb Barracks, Mullingar, and among other things described the President as a thundering disgrace.'

Liam Cosgrave was always a most accessible man and during the period that I worked for him, as what would probably now be termed Press Secretary to the Taoiseach, he dealt with good news and bad news with great equanimity. However, that was one job I would not have deliberately sought out. Immediately I had delivered the information, he got to work with his Private Secretary, Frank Murray.

Since then there have been several versions of what really happened in Mullingar, including one attributed to me, not surprisingly since I was involved with bringing the news to the Taoiseach in the first place and then dealing with what appeared to be the whole media of Ireland in the next few days. When I got back to my own offices, also in Government Buildings, the staff had already taken over fifty phone calls.

The journalist who was central to everything at Columb Barracks at all the vital times and who wrote the story was Don Lavery. He was at that time a reporter on the local paper *The Westmeath Examiner*, and is now on the newsdesk of the *Irish Independent*. He was interviewed on the twenty-fifth anniversary of the story by Gerald Barry, Producer and Director of the RTÉ 1 *This Week* radio programme. I believe from my own involvement and what I have learned down the years that this record is as accurate as you can get.

Lavery Interview with Gerald Barry

Lavery: Basically it was a visit to Mullingar by Defence Minister Paddy Donegan. It was a pretty mundane story, if you like, because I was sent to cover it in Columb Barracks in Mullingar. It was the opening of a canteen, basically, and a dining facility. The Minister arrived, and he wasn't drunk, as has been speculated since. He had something to say and he said it. He came over to me in the canteen. I had asked for a script of his speech. In fact, there was only one script available. He gave me the script and it was very dull. There was nothing in it. I gave him back the script. We were sitting down. I was sitting eight or ten inches across the dining room table from him. He stood up, threw the script in front of me and said: 'I'll give you some news for the Press.' He then launched into his speech, whereby he basically attacked the President for sending the Emergency Powers Bill to the Supreme Court. Halfway through the speech he said, very succinctly: 'In my opinion he is a thundering disgrace.'

At that, there was an army officer that I knew, sitting beside me. He kicked me very sharply on the shin, in case I had missed the importance of the remark. I hadn't. The Minister finished his speech; there was applause. He asked the senior army officer what he thought of the speech. The senior army officer said: 'Straight from the shoulder as usual, Minister.'

This was in a room full of commissioned army officers, who owed their loyalty to the President, but none of them objected. After the speech I was making my way out and an army officer approached me and said: 'The Justice Minister, Paddy Cooney, who is the local TD, would like to speak to you.' I said that was fine as long as he understood that I would report what was said. In the event I didn't meet Mr Cooney. I made my way out of the Barracks and another army officer said to me in a joke: 'We'll have to put you in handcuffs!'

Subsequent to that there was a phone call to the local newspaper where I worked, *The Westmeath Examiner*, looking for the editor. The call was made by an army officer on behalf of a politician, and I believe it was an attempt to suppress the story. But in fact, I wrote up the story and all hell broke loose at that stage.

Barry: And it eventually led to the resignation of the President who, not surprisingly, found himself grossly offended by a speech made by the Minister for Defence in front of an army of which, as you say, he was Commander-in-Chief.

Lavery: Yes, indeed. I believe there was a late attempt at an apology by the Minister to the President. The incident happened on a Monday. By the Friday the President felt that he had to resign. Basically the relationship between himself and the Minister had been, as he put it, 'irretrievably breached'. The Minister, Paddy Donegan — the government basically stood by him. He wasn't demoted at that stage. He wasn't sacked. He did write a letter of apology to the President, I understand, where he apologised for the specific words 'thundering disgrace'. But that obviously wasn't enough.

Barry: And these words 'thundering disgrace' — you must have met hundreds of people, literally hundreds of people throughout your lifetime since, who tell you that they know exactly what Paddy Donegan said and it wasn't 'thundering disgrace'; it was something very much worse. But you know the truth.

Lavery: Absolutely. I've heard very many different permutations … er … in relation to the incident … that he was an f—ing disgrace and so on. No. The exact words used were 'he's a thundering disgrace.' As I said, I was eight to ten inches from him. I was the closest person to him. I had a good shorthand note, and he later apologised for those specific words. So I'm quite happy that it was reported accurately.

Barry: It's sometimes a bizarre experience to be remembered mainly for one thing that happened in your life, and you've done so many other things both at a personal level, professional level, everything. Other things that must mean a lot more, had more significance for you and more importance for you, but this is what people remember. Is it still a part of your mind or do you mind people reminding that you were the reporter there?

Lavery: I don't. As you say, Gerry, I suppose I've been involved or covered in some way or another every major news story that's happened in the last twenty-five years. But this particular one seems to come back to haunt me at different stages. But no, I don't mind answering questions about it at all.

Bill Loughnane

Everyone in the Dáil bar has a story about the late Clare Fianna Fáil deputy Dr Bill Loughnane. Former RTÉ political correspondent Seán Duignan tells the story of having to look after a visiting American journalist, a senior editorial staff member of the *Christian Science Monitor*, who wanted to attend a Dáil sitting.

Collecting the journalist from the old Royal Hibernian Hotel in Dawson Street, Duignan escorted him across Molesworth Street, through the entrance to Leinster House, across the plinth and up to the main door, all the while having to listen to his guest's expressed hope that he would be entertained by 'a touch of old blarney and even some leprechaun-type exchanges' in the Dáil debates.

Irritated, Duignan decided to set the American straight and paused before entering the House: 'If it's blarney or shamrockery you're looking for, I'm afraid you'll be disappointed. You're in for a very sober, serious and possibly even a tedious experience here.'

But as they entered the lobby, they were greeted by the unmistakable strains of a fiddle. Skipping backwards from a pair of worried Dáil ushers, while sawing furiously away on his beloved instrument, was the redoubtable Dr Bill.

'Ah, Dr Bill, please Dr Bill,' wailed a few of his colleagues.

A broad smile spread over the American's face.

Said Duignan: 'There was nothing I could say to the Yank except "Enjoy yourself" while I headed straight for the bar.'

12. How it All Began

Mayor of New York

On a wet Wednesday in March, Aidan and Frank Durkin had a visit from their parents in Bohola, County Roscommon. Nothing unusual about that. During my time in St Nathy's College, Ballaghaderreen, Wednesday was a half-day and there were always some parents up for a visit.

What made this visit unusual was what the Durkin parents brought with them. For in along with the cakes, sweets, chocolate and GAA newspaper cuttings was a bagful of election lapel badges!

I can still remember the badge in all its detail. It was about 5 centimetres in diameter, with a background of the American flag in full colour, and superimposed on this, in black and white, a head-and-shoulders picture of Bill O'Dwyer. Aidan Durkin had a badge for everyone in his class, including me, and Frank had one for everyone in his class. In addition, because my bed was next to Aidan's in the dormitory, I also qualified for a full colour poster, which was more or less an enlarged version of the lapel badge with some extra wording.

After that we were all part of an election campaign. It didn't matter that the election was for Mayor of New York, or that it was between the Democrats and Republicans, of whose politics we were totally ignorant. After all, Bill O'Dwyer was an uncle of two of our schoolmates and a past pupil of St Nathy's, and he was running for what, as far as we were concerned, was the job just below that of the President of the United States! What more did anyone want to know? Furthermore, most of the boarders then came from the emigration counties of Mayo and Sligo, and knew more about the streets of New York than those of Dublin city. I myself had twenty-nine first cousins in New York, as against four in Ireland, and those three were the children of a returned Yank!

So we wore our badges and we backed our man until we saw Bill O'Dwyer safely through the primaries and, in a way we did not understand, becoming Mayor as the Democrat candidate was a formality.

St Nathy's

Even without a favourite son like Bill O'Dwyer, we loved our politics in St Nathy's. Not that the college did much to encourage our interest or improve our knowledge. The teaching of history stopped dead at the turn of the nineteenth century when it was just becoming interesting. There were no civics classes. There were no newspapers allowed in the college and no radio. Even the most likely of the teachers could not be cajoled into political debate, while they pontificated on everything else.

Despite this lack of source material and adequate briefing, we still loved to talk and to argue politics, and in this we were only reflecting what was happening at home around the firesides of Sligo and Mayo, at the crossroads and outside the church gates on a Sunday morning.

We were uninhibited by our lack of knowledge of the social and economic issues. In that, we were not much different from the Dáil deputies of the day. At that time politics was very simple — you were for de Valera or you were against him. The nearest we got to seeing a live politician during our college days was the odd glimpse of James Dillon, who lived in the town and ran a business there. Truth to tell, we had more interest in the bread he baked for us in Monica Duff's than in the undoubted brilliance of his oratory!

The political arguments amongst the boarders were regular and robust. At election times in the great world outside, they became more frequent and more furious. Amongst the more regular and dogmatic contributors was a John Healy from Charlestown, County Mayo. He was a year behind me, but already he had made his career choice. When he left St Nathy's, he was going to be a journalist, and he couldn't wait.

After St Nathy's, John and myself went our separate ways, but seven years later we were together again in the newsroom of the *Irish Press* in Burgh Quay, then the best newsroom in the business. And a further four years on, we were together in the *Irish Times* offices in D'Olier Street, with John as the editor of the *Sunday Review* and myself as news editor.

This was a tabloid paper of *The Irish Times*, with a circulation of 180,000. We set our target to push that circulation above 200,000. And in seeking ways to do it, we went back to our experience in St Nathy's and the interest that we knew existed in politics in the West and all over the country in rural areas.

Those political discussions that we had in St Nathy's, as we sheltered by the ball alley from the cold winds coming in from 'Bacagh', may not have done much to advance political thought in the country. But I like to think that it may have led to a very significant change in the way politics was reported and presented to the Irish people.

Starting Out

For what precise reason I don't know, but I decided I would try to make a career in journalism. Naturally I didn't expect immediate success, but I was taken aback by the response of one wise editor (somehow they all become 'wise editors'). He told me that I had already made my first big mistake, and that was

> not to be born within cycling distance or better still walking distance of the offices of a local paper. There is no school of journalism in this country so you have to start as a trainee or 'cub' reporter, as I prefer to call it. The trouble about that is that the wages we can pay you wouldn't get you half decent digs. I'm sure if I went out with you there on the street, I'd find at least one potential Pulitzer prize-winner who had to give up without even getting his name on a Christmas lights story.

What I wanted desperately was a start, and this wasn't easy in the hungry early 1950s. Finally I got a promise of a job through football contacts but I would have to wait patiently for the best part of six months. So I took the cattle boat to England, where most of my class already were. My friends directed me to Manchester. I got digs in Irlam, and a job in the nearby co-operative wholesale society, candle-making, with good overtime coming up to Christmas. My neighbours from Aclare, especially Luke Kildunne, the brother Mike Joe, and Andy Hegarty who wrote me a poem of welcome, all made me feel at home.

This was rugby league country, despite all the big soccer clubs around, and because I was a county footballer with Sligo, my flatmates talked the local club of Cadishead and Irlam into giving me a trial. Things worked out better then we expected. I got the occasional game and expenses, and my 'handlers' got free membership of the snooker club, where they could play anytime.

I was referred to in the papers as Ted Nealow. I imagine it was a typographical error, but my friends put out the word that it was to protect my amateur status — no less — because the Gaelic football ban on playing 'foreign' sports was still in operation.

Back in Ireland, my start was with the *Monaghan and Dundalk Argus* under a great editor, Fintan Faulkner, who later became editor of the *Irish Press*. I resumed Gaelic football, and this enabled me to build up very good contacts in the border areas where many of the players were gardaí, on special border duties. However, the ambition of nearly all young, ambitious journalists at that time was to get a job with one of the national newspapers in Dublin.

My opening came in the *Irish Press*. I was interviewed by the editor, Jim McGuinness, later to become editor of RTÉ News, who encouraged me to keep on playing Gaelic football, and by Bill Redmond, chief news editor, who encouraged me to practise shorthand. The job was mine. I know that I am biased, but I believe that, certainly on big stories, the newsroom of the *Irish Press* was the best there was at that time. Because of my experience of the border area and the contacts I had made during my time as a trainee, I was often sent on assignment there.

13. Belfast – The Missing Years

One of my regrets is that I never got to know Belfast as I should have. While it was always in the news — unfortunately often for the wrong reasons — I stayed there for only one significant period as a journalist and then it was filling in for a colleague in the *Irish Press* offices. As a politician and Minister for Arts and Culture, I was there on just two occasions, the second to visit Cultra Folk Park, and, if I recollect rightly, this was a visit organised by my own department.

I returned from Cultra convinced that we needed something of a similar nature in the South. It so happened that the perfect location existed in my own constituency of Sligo–Leitrim! The ideal situation would be for the State to purchase Lissadell House as a headquarters for the National Folk Collection following years of homeless neglect, including 'detention' in Daingean, County Offaly. As Minister, I was able to do something about that. The grounds and the magnificent farm and engineering buildings at Lissadell could be developed for exhibitions and for Cultra-style developments. As a local Dáil Deputy, I had kept in contact over a long period with Sir Jocelyn Gore-Booth, but because of developments elsewhere the house had been taken off the market at that time.

The cost of all this is the kind of thing a Minister for Finance these days, or even then, would lose in a tot. However, the government didn't have a 'tosser' and the opportunity is now gone, to my great regret. The National Folk Collection is elsewhere and being very well cared for and displayed.

If you didn't know Belfast well, as I didn't, the next best thing was to know James Kelly, doyen of Irish journalism, whose autobiography, *Bonfires on the Hillside*, is a fascinating commentary on the Northern Ireland political scene. For fifty years he was Northern Editor of Irish Independent newspapers, a correspondent for the *Manchester Guardian* and the United Press of America. And he is still writing.

JAMES KELLY

Dev in Belfast

Before Mr de Valera 'went to the Park' as President of Ireland in 1959, he was invited to Queen's University Belfast, an unusual and hopeful event in view of his recent history as a man who was banned from the North for many years, and regarded by many Northern loyalists as the devil incarnate. There was a tremendous turn-out at the spacious Whitla Hall for the occasion and Dev had every reason to be pleased with the reception he received. He was accompanied, as always, by his faithful lieutenant and 'minder', Mr Frank Aitken.

I was curious to meet Aitken, one-time leader of the Northern Division of the old IRA and a native of South Armagh, but when I was introduced I found him dry and taciturn, with little to say beyond an occasional 'Yes, yes' — one of the most ill-at-ease politicians I have ever met. This was in complete contrast to Dev himself, who met us in an ante-room

and was quite chatty, charming the Belfast newspapermen with his warmth and friendliness.

It was a historic occasion and the packed audience
was agog to hear what Dev, a survivor of the 1916
Rising, would say to a Belfast gathering and a mixed
one at that. 'It is', he said, 'not the first time I have
come to Belfast.' He paused and we wondered if he
was going to tell about his experiences in Belfast Gaol.
'I came here as a young student. It was the Twelfth of
July,' he continued, and the crowd laughed. So he was
going to tell us of his reaction to the great march of
the Orangemen on that day of days in Belfast when
everything stops for the besashed brethren parading
behind massed bands and the big drums. But no, Dev
was keeping us in suspense. He had not seen or heard
the Orangemen and their music, 'The Sash', 'The Lily-
O', 'Derry's Walls' and 'No Surrender', or even 'Kick
the Pope'.

He confessed that he had spent the day at McArt's
Fort on Cave Hill, communing with the spirits of the
1798 Presbyterian United Irishmen, Wolfe Tone,
Henry Joy McCracken and the rest. The crowd gasped
and broke into chattering reaction, and no wonder.
Here was one of the mistakes of history. No Southern
Irish politician facing the realities of a dissident
Protestant population immersed in different folk-
ways and traditions can afford to ignore this
manifestation of the tribalism that gave the colour of
orange to the Irish Tricolour. The symbolism of the
flag is white for peace between the Orange and the
Green. Was that not a mistake anyhow, a recognition
of the division? Was the old Hibernian flag of green
surmounted by the golden harp not a more inspiring
national emblem? The symbolism of the Tricolour
was lost on the Northern Protestants anyhow. They
insisted on calling it a flag of 'green, white and yellow'

and when it was banned by Sir Dawson Bates he made the mistake of so designating it. This enabled James McSparran QC to drive a 'coach-and-horses' through a prosecution in an Armagh court where a defendant was charged with the illegal display of the Tricolour. Thereafter cowardly-sounding 'Yellow' was altered in the Special Powers Act to loyal 'Orange'.

Republican dreamers in Dublin who talk nostalgically about the Presbyterians in the North one day awakening to their great Republican heritage should come North on 12 July but go straight to Royal Avenue and forget about Cave Hill. Better to face the truth and take it from there. In other words, don't make the mistake Dev made.

When Prime Minister Terence O'Neill set about organising Ulster societies in the United States from the descendants of Washington's 'Scotch-Irish' from Ulster, he had his critics at home. The late James Faulkner, the affable linen shirt manufacturer, father of Brian Faulkner, and whom I knew very well, met me one morning in a Fountain Street coffee house and made me laugh at his reaction to the Premier's 'Scotch-Irish' plans. 'What's he talking about?' he snorted. 'Sure his bloody ancestors drove them out of Ulster.'

Another time when Dev was due to travel North for the unveiling of a memorial to Roger Casement at Murlough Bay near Ballycastle, we were tipped off that Northern Republicans were preparing a hot reception for him. Republicans like Jimmy Steele and his friends decided that it was time to confront the 'Chief' over his tough treatment of the IRA during the war years when there had been executions, internments and deaths on hunger strike. The death of Belfast man Seán McCaughey after 23 days without food or water at Portlaoise Prison particularly rankled and the plan was to shout Dev down when he rose to speak. Dev and the organisers were blissfully unaware of the plot to cause such disruption that he would 'never dare to show his face in the North again'. We were told the night before that this would be the end for the 'big fellow'.

We were close up to the platform with our pens poised, but whether it was cold feet, the enthusiastic reception of the crowd or the semi-religious background to the memorial unveiling, the expected rumpus never materialised. We could see some of the Republican demonstrators moving among the spectators but when we caught their eyes, they shook their heads and later confessed that they had come to the conclusion on the spot that the uproar they had planned would not have been appropriate in the circumstances!

The occasion passed quietly, Mr de Valera making his usual impassioned appeal on behalf of the Irish language which hard-line republicans dared not disrupt. Dev never knew how close he came to one of the most embarrassing moments in his long life.

West of the Bann

Catch-phrases that I invented were often quoted back to me by people in the street long after I had forgotten them. Government policy at that time seemed to be to cram all incoming new industry into the Protestant heartland within a thirty-mile radius of Belfast and to neglect the majority Nationalist areas on the far side of the River Bann and Lough Neagh. For convenience I lumped the neglected industrial desert of Derry, Tyrone and Fermanagh together in my weekly column of the *Sunday Independent* as the forgotten region 'West of the Bann'. The description caught the imagination, and thereafter Brookeborough heard plenty about his policy of allowing 'West of the Bann' to languish in the western mists.

The Old Stormont

Stormont was a free-and-easy place for newspapermen, with a minimum of protocol. We could move around the lobbies unchallenged and speak to Members or Ministers in the bar or the dining room without any of the ceremony and fuss associated with Westminster or Leinster House, Dublin. Visiting pressmen from Dublin and London were astonished at the facilities we enjoyed. We often wished that the good crack in the Bar between political opponents could have been transferred to the floor of the Commons where, to maintain public attitudes, the exchanges could appear so bitter.

Holding Hands on Royal Avenue

There was a lot of laughter too. Tommy Henderson in his day provided a lot of fun. I still recall vividly his memorable threat to the Government about the risen people of 'Ulster'. Waving his finger at the front bench he declared: 'The day is coming when the lion of progress will march down Royal Avenue, hand in hand with the floodgates of democracy!'

Billy Douglas and 'Senator' Paisley

Billy Douglas was one of the great power-brokers and 'Mr Fixit' of the Glengall Street headquarters of the Unionist Party. When I met Billy Douglas after a

Radio Telifís Éireann confrontation in Dublin, he was in a reminiscent mood in the reception room. He confessed that the greatest mistake of his life was to send a young man named Ian K. Paisley packing when he came to Glengall Street seeking the Unionist nomination for a vacant Stormont Senatorship.

Paisley had been making a name for himself as a rabble-rouser in a local Dock election, appearing for the first time as 'election agent' in a hotly contested marginal seat. Douglas considered that some elderly wheel-horse Unionist had a greater claim for membership of the Senate than this young upstart, who before many years had rocked the whole Unionist edifice by founding not alone his own breakaway Free Presbyterian Church but also his own Democratic Unionist Party.

Billy groaned audibly between drinks, 'When I think of the trouble we could have avoided, it makes me want to weep,' he said.

[James Kelly, *Bonfires on the Hillside*, Fountain Books, 1995]

Football Medal

As far as honours are concerned, I'm by no means a cynic. It's just that I don't seem to have been around very much when they were being handed out! The few I've got, I appreciate; in particular being made a Freeman of the Borough of Sligo. On the Roll of Honour I'm next to Westlife!

I was very honoured and surprised to get a French Government award, *Commandant dans l'Ordre des Arts et des Lettres*, in 1985 when I was Minister for Arts and Culture. It came on the nomination of the French Socialist Minister for Arts, Jack Lang, arising out of work I had done with him in the European Community Council of Ministers. It came with a distinctive lapel button and sash. For twenty-five years I constantly wore the lapel button and during all that time scarcely anyone ever noticed it, or asked what it represented!

———

The sash was a different matter, just a little bit smaller than what the Orangemen wear on 12 July. No one could miss it. However, the problem this time was that there was never an opportunity for me to wear it. I needed a picture opportunity, and the inauguration in Dublin Castle of Mary Robinson as Úachtarán na hÉireann seemed to provide a half-opening.

The briefing from the Protocol Section of the Department of the Taoiseach clearly indicated 'No medals', so anything official was out. However, I knew that a number of my colleagues would be gathering in Leinster House before the ceremonies. The office next door to mine was Jimmy Deenihan's.

At the appropriate time, after lining up four or five of my colleagues including Deputy Theresa Ahern of Tipperary South, I went in with my sash to Jimmy and, adopting the most casual attitude, asked him to help with fastening the clips.

Deputy Deenihan examined it from all angles. Then came the question: 'Jaysus, Nealon, what did you get this for — playing football? You'd think you were waiting for the Artane Boys' Band to strike up!'

That is the kind of thing that a Kerryman with five All Ireland medals in his pocket can say to a Sligo man and get away with it.

A Night on the Border

Lieutenant-Colonel Matt Feehan was the unlikely choice of editor when *The Sunday Press* was launched on All Ireland Hurling Sunday, 1949. As he told his deputy editor, Douglas Gageby, he knew nothing about newspapers and had never previously been in a newspaper office before his own! Feehan could be described as a 'product' of the Emergency. He moved quickly through the ranks of the army, gaining a reputation as a man of exceptional organisational ability and endurance. 'My men will march,' he is reported to have said when, after a tough two weeks of exercises, he was offered transport for the final fifteen miles back to base. Much to the lasting loss of army lore, it is not recorded what was the response of the men who had to do the marching, even if the Colonel did join them.

The launch of *The Sunday Press* was the first major expansion for the Burgh Quay newspaper publishing house and there is no doubt that the decision on the choice of editor was made by the man with total control of all matters, Éamon de Valera. In his well-researched book, Mark O'Brien described Colonel Feehan as a staunch republican and quotes him as saying that he would never cross the Border 'unless at the head of a battalion'. Whatever self-imposed limitations he might have on his own movements in the island, he had no such limitations on where his reporters might go. Anywhere there was a prospect of a good story, Colonel Feehan's attitude was to be there, gather up the essential elements and then 'splash' it.

Working for him on *The Sunday Press*, the editor had a small but talented and fiercely loyal staff. I was amongst five to eight reporters in the *Irish Press* newsroom called in to help on Saturdays — print days. The reward was £2 10s for an eight-hour shift, from four to midnight, very attractive considering that, after deductions, the entire weekly wage from the *Irish Press* would be £8 to £9. We may not have had the same loyalty to Colonel Feehan as his regular staff, but we always turned up.

Our main obligation was to be around just in case there were major news developments of any sort. If you preferred to do your waiting in the White Horse pub or Mulligan's, that was alright as long as the news editor knew where to get you at the vital times. Then after 11.30 pm as the mood moved him, Colonel Feehan would declare 'Job up' and rattle out with his knuckles on the sub-editors' desk 'Many Young Men of Twenty'.

Amongst a select group called in every Saturdays was Seán Cryan from Roscommon, a crime reporter, who looked like a garda and sometimes allowed himself to be mistaken for one to advance a news story. Among his duties on Saturday night was to go to Dublin Airport and, by hook or by crook, get hold of a few copies of the Irish editions of the English Sunday papers being flown in for the Irish market. These frequently carried useful 'pickings' that could be rewritten for the later editions of *The Sunday Press*. Regularly one or other of the Fleet Street papers would have a major story, particularly on IRA activities, and the exclusive nature would suggest that it had originated in the journalistic pool of the day. We would always be disappointed if the rewritten version for *The Sunday Press* didn't turn out to be that bit better than the original exclusive.

Others on the 'Colonel's shilling' included Michael Mills, who later became the first Ombudsman in the State, and Joe Jennings, who was afterwards Director of Government Information Services.

Despite his lack of experience in newspapers, Colonel Feehan quickly proved that he could do one thing better than anyone else in the country at that time — sell newspapers, or maybe produce newspapers that people wanted to buy. I believe it was a skilful mix of the two, with the emphasis, for the first time in Irish newspapers, as much on the presentation as on the content. Whatever it was, it worked and sales soared weekly to around 350,000, the largest for any paper in Ireland at that time.

———

One Saturday evening in 1956 I arrived at the Burgh Quay offices around four o'clock to check in for my *Sunday Press* shift, very pleased to be on the roster. As soon as I came through the doorway, the deputy news editor, George Kerr, shouted over,

'Don't take off your coat, Ted. You're going to the Border.'

The Border area was volatile, with the IRA and several splinter groups operating on both sides. So it was no great surprise that *The Sunday Press* was sending a reporter up there. What was a surprise was the brief.

George Kerr, a Border man himself, from Clones, County Monaghan, explained very carefully to me that this was the personal decision of Matt Feehan. I was to go to the Border along with a photographer, and then, starting in the Carrickmacross, Crossmaglen and Castleblayney area, begin moving west, keeping at all times on the Southern side, and travel as far as Ballyconnell or maybe even as far as Bundoran — all would depend on what the approaching daylight would dictate. Along the way we were to call at all the major Garda barracks to check if there were any developments. Otherwise, it was just drive — a mini-Border circuit.

I asked George Kerr if he had some tip-off, some information that could not be given to me until I was in position in the Border area.

'No, nothing at all like that,' George explained. 'Colonel Feehan hasn't been satisfied with our coverage in the Border area on Saturday nights. He thinks that the answer might be this circuit of the Border. Personally I think it's crazy, but you didn't hear that from me.'

The photographer assigned to the Border trip was Seán Bourke, son of Deputy Paddy Bourke and a staff member of the *Irish Press* art department. Seán was good company and an enthusiast about virtually any story. He was a realist who didn't expect a masterpiece every time the shutters clicked. A car was waiting in the *Irish Press* garage under the archways of the Tara Street railway line. We agreed that this Border circuit was a daft enterprise, probably of a dimension we had not experienced before. We got into the car and headed north.

We discussed our instructions as we travelled towards Carrickmacross. If anything were to happen along the Border

that night, we felt, the best possible way to miss it was to do what
we were now doing. At that time there was no way our car could
receive or send communications. With luck, inquiries at the
major Garda stations along the Border could help, or they could
go the other way, depending on the mood of the sergeant in
charge. As an alternative to the 'circuit', we felt we could base
ourselves centrally and be in a position to act on any
information we might get from our office in Dublin. There was
one further consideration. Only a relatively short time
previously I had worked as a reporter on the *Monaghan Argus*
newspaper and I also had played Gaelic football with the local
Monaghan Harps. Several of the players were gardaí on Border
duty.

With the encouragement of Seán Bourke, I contacted
Colonel Feehan, suggesting the changes. First of all, in typical
Colonel Feehan fashion, he took full responsibility for the
operation we were on. It was his idea. He accepted the problems
that we had pointed out and he was willing to change. 'Just pick
your base, let me know and keep in contact,' he said.

We decided on Monaghan town as our base, again because it
was the area I knew best and because it was a major centre in
the garda surveillance of the Border at the time. Our first call
was on the Garda station on Plantation Road. There were a lot
of gardaí around but no hectic activity.

We booked into the Westenra Hotel in the Diamond. From
there, I took the precaution of contacting a friend, Des Benson,
in Killeshandra, County Cavan. Des was a correspondent for a
number of newspapers and frequently worked with the Fleet
Street journalists on Border duty. He was also a goalkeeper with
the Cavan County team, so was extremely well known. It was
said about him that nothing flew in Cavan without Des Benson
being told of it, except maybe the odd crow going for its lunch
in Monaghan. Des had nothing definite to tell me but he had
heard rumours of a lot of garda traffic in the Three-Mile-House
area, not far from Monaghan town.

Things began to change rapidly after that. Maurice Hickey, a very senior reporter with the *Irish Independent*, walked into the Westenra. We exchanged greetings but nothing else. It was obvious to us that Maurice was there on a specific assignment. We also knew, as did most Dublin journalists, that the *Irish Independent* and particularly the *Sunday Independent* had exceptionally good contacts within Dublin Castle. The next arrival, shortly afterwards, was Jack Keneally, a rising star in *The Sunday Express* team covering Ireland north and south. He was accompanied by Cliff Beddell, a wartime cameraman with a big reputation. They had come from Belfast or from Enniskillen and we guessed they had arrived with specific information, probably originating from the same source as the *Sunday Independent*. While I was personally friendly with them, we were there in Monaghan as competitors.

Although I was still lacking vital details, all the signs were of some major Border development. Word was getting through also that the major British papers were honing in on the story. It was time for the three reporters in Monaghan to get together to see if we could do a deal. They had the advantage of precise information and I had the advantage of local knowledge.

The negotiations were quick because of the other papers being alerted. The deal done was that they would make available the information they had to me and I would not embark on any solo runs with the contacts I had and I would keep them informed on what I picked up.

First the information. It was precise and it was startling. The *Sunday Independent* and *The Sunday Express* had learned hours earlier that thirteen men were in occupation of a farmhouse near Three-Mile-House, an area in the north of County Monaghan near the Fermanagh border. Already the gardaí had surrounded the house, at a distance, and were to demand the surrender of the armed men at a specific time in the early morning. Most of these details were new information for my paper, *The Sunday Press*. I filled them in, without disclosing my own source ('the phones are leaky' was an excuse accepted all round).

Colonel Feehan immediately took the decision to hold the front page for the story, irrespective of how this would disrupt his overall distribution schedule. If the timings given to the *Sunday Independent* and *The Sunday Express* were correct, there was still a couple of hours to go before the showdown.

Maurice Hickey, Jack Keneally and myself were now working together. We decided on two things — to keep a regular watch on the Garda Station and to drive by the occupied house, situated, we understood, in the mountains.

From our visits to the Garda station we noticed a rapid build-up in personnel and, looking under the gates, we also saw what appeared to be army vehicles, in addition to those of the gardaí. We then set out for Three-Mile-House. I knew how to get to the Gaelic football pitch, known as Iodine Park. After that, we started making enquiries. A cyclist was able to give us all the details we needed and was especially helpful when I told him that I had personal experience of playing in Iodine Park. I mentioned a name. 'He's still around,' the cyclist said, 'but he's retired now from football, so that's good news for the noses; not too good for the bone-setters!' In giving us directions, he naturally put us on the shortest road. After locating the house, we did a quick return to Monaghan Town. Only just in time! Because we had failed to keep the arranged watch on Monaghan Garda station, the convoy had been able to slip through a special gateway.

When we arrived back at The Diamond in Monaghan Town, a young garda rushed over to me.

'Are you Ted Nealon?' he asked.

'Yes.'

'I was asked to tell you: "They're gone".'

So was he, gone also, when I turned around again.

'Three-Mile-House?' Seán Bourke shouted from the car to the only uniformed man now left in The Diamond. 'Are we right?'

'I couldn't say you're wrong,' the garda replied and quickly left the scene.

We were heading back to the farmhouse we had reconnoitred a short time previously, confident that we must be right, although a bit worried that there were no signs of the lights of a large convoy of vehicles. With the local knowledge we had collected, we were in fact travelling a different, shorter road than the gardaí. The lead car of the convoy and Seán Bourke's car met within yards of the farmhouse entrance and blocked all movement.

With the thirteen men still inside and with the gardaí and the army taking up positions close to the house, it was a highly dangerous situation, which I felt could have gone dreadfully wrong. The gardaí quickly sorted out the road blockage by heaving the *Irish Press* black Volkswagen onto the side of a ditch. That enabled them to get their men into position and to move the journalists, reporters and photographers up the road, out of danger from any exchange of fire that might develop. Fortunately, amongst the gardaí was Detective-Sergeant Christy MacNamee from Clontibret Garda station, whom I knew through local football.

'Jaysus! Ted Nealon! What are you doing in the mountains of Knockawhillen?'

Christy then found us a place for our own safety, for observations of the farmhouse and for pictures, depending on developments.

The immediate siege didn't last very long. Obviously the men inside had already made their decision not to embark on any resistance. They walked into the custody of the gardaí and their waiting vehicles. They were detained in Monaghan barracks.

My job had now switched to phoning in to Burgh Quay the developments in the mountains and within half an hour the presses were running and the distribution lorries revving up. Seán Bourke was on his way back to Dublin with his precious flashbulb shots that would be run in the newspapers on many occasions on the following days.

I'm told there was no 'Job up' from Colonel Feehan that morning. Instead, he was out in the streets urging the circulation and distribution men to greater efforts in the hope of clawing back some of the time lost as a result of the long stake-out in the mountains around Knockawhillen. He had his 'splash'. He was now switched back to sales.

The Border Campaign of the IRA

In December 1956 the Prime Minister of Northern Ireland, Lord Brookeborough, was appearing live on the BBC *Panorama* programme with presenter Richard Dimbleby. As the programme got underway, Lord Brookeborough told Dimbleby that he had received a message only a few minutes earlier that an IRA attack was actually taking place on a police car near his home in Lisnaskea, County Fermanagh.

'At this moment?' Dimbleby asked.

'At this very moment,' was Brookeborough's reply. 'I don't know exactly what is happening, but I may later....' This was television history being made: the Prime Minister, live, with the latest news. Listening in the TV lounge in the Westenra Hotel in Monaghan were about twenty or thirty Fleet Street and Dublin journalists who were in the area to cover the IRA Border campaign, with roughly the same numbers in a hotel in Enniskillen. Soon both hotels were deserted, with the media heading for Lisnaskea. I travelled from Monaghan and in Lisnaskea met up with my colleague Eileen O'Brien, who ran the *Irish Press* office in Belfast and who could handle the tough endurance trial along the Border with the best. We did the sensible thing for once and phoned in a joint report.

It gives some idea of the media interest being generated by the activities of the IRA and a number of splinter groups that within an hour of Lord Brookeborough's revelations on television, there were at least sixty media people gathered in a small town on the Fermanagh/Monaghan border. This is the heart of Churchill's 'dreary steeples'.

The terminology being used by all the media in reports was of a Border campaign, though the editor Tim Pat Coogan didn't regard it as the sustained, continuous activity that could be called a campaign. For him, it was a series of 'incidents', another unfortunate word used in the media at the time. Some of these incidents were in parts of Northern Ireland, well away from the Border. These would most likely be reported by local correspondents for the *Irish Press* newsroom. On one such occasion I was with a group of reporters processing the 'copy' as it came in. Sitting beside me was Michael Mills, later to become the first Ombudsman.

Passing through the newsroom was Seán Cronin, a journalist who was an important link in the production of the *Evening Press*. He stopped for a moment as he passed by and said to the group: 'Great stuff, lads. Keep the copy flowing,' and went on his way.

'You know who that is?' Michael Mills said to me.

'No.'

'He's the Chief of Staff of the IRA.'

There was a lot of media speculation at this time about the possibility of the IRA ceasing activities over the Christmas period and making an announcement to that effect. With the information available to the *Irish Press*, the belief was that there would be a ceasefire. This meant that I could get down to my native Coolrecull, Aclare, in south County Sligo to spend the holidays with my father.

On my way back to Dublin, I heard of the attack on Brookeborough Barracks in County Fermanagh and of the deaths of Fergal O'Hanlon from Monaghan Town and Seán South from Garryowen, County Limerick.

Fergal O'Hanlon I knew very well. When I had worked as a reporter on *The Monaghan Argus* some years earlier, we were both members of the Monaghan Harps football team. Fergal, aged about eighteen, was showing great potential. He called occasionally at my office, where we often talked football with Gerry Brennan, a star Monaghan player, who had an office next door. It was a particularly good time for the Harps, who lost only one match through the season.

My first call back in Dublin was to the newsroom of the *Irish Press* where the deputy news editor, George Kerr, immediately approached me.

'You'll have to go back again to the Border, and I know that this is something you're not going to like. You have to call to the O'Hanlon home in Monaghan, to try to get a photograph of Fergal. All the newspapers are looking for it and the editor thinks you should have a try because of the football and the friendship. Do you think you have any chance?'

'Yes, I do.'

Then George proceeded in the typical style of a news editor. 'Would it be possible to get one in time for the country [early] edition of the *Irish Press*?'

Five yards away in the newsroom was my locker with a folder of Monaghan Harps footballers celebrating their championship win. Fergal O'Hanlon had sent it to me nearly a year earlier, at the club's request.

14. The Backbencher Years

A lot of coverage of Irish politics in the national media is now by way of comment and opinion. Dáil deputies and senators frequently complain that much of their important work, especially in the tough grind of committees, is more or less ignored in the newspapers. When I first worked on covering national politics, with the *Irish Press* group in the 1950s, the balance was much different. Politics got lots of space, but mostly by way of straight reports and quotations. 'Mr de Valera said' or 'Mr John A. Costello said' and so on down the line. Each of the four national daily papers sent four reporters to Leinster House on Dáil-sitting days. All the Irish papers worked on a pool basis in ten-minute shifts. In addition, those of us working for the *Irish Press* had to send in verbatim coverage of everything de Valera uttered.

Although this kind of saturation coverage gave readers a very good picture of the way the government and the Houses of the Oireachtas worked, of its nature it made for dull reading, except for the occasional time when there was genuine confrontation on the floor of the House. Change of style was inevitable but slow in coming. Although I was directly involved myself, I think it is fair to claim that the introduction in *The Sunday Review* in 1961 of a regular political column with a different style was a major influence in the change.

The Sunday Review was published by *The Irish Times*. It had a respectable circulation of around 180,000, but a minimum of at least 200,000 was regarded as essential for survival at a time when the national economy was in difficulty, the budgets of the advertisers were being slashed and the new RTÉ television channel would be taking an ever bigger slice of what was there. *The Sunday Review* had already the red-top tabloid format but, unlike the British tabloids, there was no question in the Ireland of the day of chasing the extra readers needed through the use of scantily clad page 3 girls. After all, this was before sex came to Ireland via *The Late, Late Show*. Moreover, in parts of rural Ireland anything coming out of D'Olier Street was still regarded by some with a certain amount of suspicion, and *The Sunday Review* had been burned outside one church where the curate didn't agree with some of the newspaper's contents.

The Sunday paper market was already well catered for, although the English Sundays had nothing like the penetration or circulations they now have. In addition to *The Sunday Review*, there was *The Sunday Press*, with at one-time huge sales of over 350,000 and the *Sunday Independent*, also with enormous sales and much better roots and loyalties than any of the other titles. *The Sunday Review* needed fundamental changes to make any progress in its challenge to these giants. All sorts of ideas were introduced, including a gossip column by the distinguished author and *Irish Times* literary editor Terence de Vere White! The most significant change, however, came in political coverage.

John Healy, one of the best journalists in the business, was editor of *The Sunday Review*; I was news editor. John believed very strongly that new readers could be won over with a radically different style of covering Irish politics. Much more was needed on personalities, on the behind-the-scenes manoeuvrings that frequently went unreported, on the gossip surrounding the people who led the country, on personal animosities within party leaderships, all the things that feature in the papers of today.

This led to the launching in *The Sunday Review* of a new weekly column, 'Inside Politics', by Backbencher. It was written by John Healy with, initially, a significant input by myself. Later the column was transferred to *The Irish Times*. It ran there for many years and had, I believe, a considerable influence on the political developments of the time. It was often controversial; it was always entertaining. I'm sure John would like me to add that it was also splendidly and unashamedly biased. Because of the Backbencher by-line to the column, there was a fairly widely held but mistaken belief in the early *Sunday Review* days that it was being written by a serving member of the Dáil. This belief was being encouraged by us on promotional grounds. There was, indeed, a very well-informed insider politician who greatly helped the column to make a quick impact.

It soon became the column for politicians to be mentioned in. We were inundated with information from all sides of the Dáil, material designed to help or hurt in about equal measure. All parties were worried about the leaks to Backbencher from inside sources. Indeed, Fine Gael set up a committee of three wise men to see if they could stop the flow or identify its sources. We heard about this and commented on it the next Sunday. When the committee chairman, Gerry Sweetman, assembled his members in Leinster House on the following Tuesday, he opened with the words 'Well, which of us is Backbencher?'

Our favourite comment on the early days of the Backbencher column came from a wonderful lady who looked after press, publicity, library and just about everything else at the time in the Fine Gael headquarters in Hume Street, Dublin: 'I like Backbencher,' she said. 'It's equally offensive to all sides.'

I have chosen the following extracts from the Backbencher Column to give readers a flavour of those times.

The House of Groome

Next week will be a busy week in the Dáil. It will also be a busy week in Groome's Hotel, 8 Cavendish Row, Dublin. It is not a coincidence. For when the Dáil is busy, Groome's Hotel is extra busy.

The casual tourist drinking in the comfortable lounge might be pardoned for thinking that, at times, he has stumbled on a meeting of Fianna Fáil.

For in a hotel that even in the slack season is busy, the well-known party men are invariably to be found there.

The House of Groome is also patronised handsomely by the acting fraternity, headed by the Gate people across the road, as well as many of the Abbey set.

What of the politicians? On a good night you could meet most of the bright young men of the Lemass government. Neil Blaney, long before his marriage, found it a congenial place and a home from his Donegal home.

Brian Lenihan, who knows a good hotel, if only because his father owns one, is a patron of Groome's — splitting his patronage with the Dolphin, the haunt of his practising barrister days.

The Minister for Justice, Charles J. Haughey, occasionally drops in to meet and talk quietly with the politicians and the actors. So does Donogh O'Malley. And they can do so in the knowledge that they can be safe from the lobbyists who invariably seek to attach themselves to men in public life.

How did this small hotel (its rateable valuation a mere £118, as compared with the Gresham's £4000-odd, just a taxi-rank whistle down the street) achieve the 'Cabinet-ranking' distinction it holds today?

Granted the food and drink are both excellent. The service is courteous, efficient and discreet. The building, while laying no great claims to architectural splendour, radiates comfort and solidity.

The same may be said for Matt Donnelly's place a few doors above Groome's, and for hundreds of others in the country.

What then remains to make it 'The Scene-Stealer's' Club? We must look beyond. It is there we will find the quietly powerful figure of mine host, Joseph Groome.

Joe Groome, as everybody calls him, is a man of many talents, exercised with the discreetness of the family doctor. On the note heading of the Fianna Fáil party newspaper he appears as Joint Hon. Secretary. On the note heading of the Irish Tourist Association, you will find his name as a director. He is a director, too, of the Irish Hospitals Commission.

But all those roles are as nothing compared with the influence he wields in the inner circle of the Fianna Fáil organisation. Here he is the confidant and adviser of the men who govern.

Like most big men, he rarely raises his voice. He is a patient listener and sifts the facts of any case with the silent ease of an IBM computer. He does not tire easily and can suffer a bore with unlimited patience.

And he carries on the kindness and generosity his mother started when she went into the bed-and-breakfast business in Cavendish Row many, many years ago.

He is helped in all this by his charming wife. She, too, has the tact of a top-ranking diplomat and can use it, whether on a European diplomat or an aspiring *Comhairle Ceantair* bod from Tullyesker.

[From *The Sunday Review*, 15 July 1962. Backbencher Column]

My Fan from Offaly

I am told Mr Joe Groome, like most Fianna Fáil men, is almost as avid a reader of this column as the Minister for Justice, Mr Charles J. Haughey. Last Sunday he saw something of its polling power too.

On Sunday last, with thousands of Leinster men cramming the city for the big game at Croke Park, the House of Groome did big business. As usual.

One man wearing the Offaly colours walked in, found himself a table with some difficulty, pulled out his copy of *Sunday Review*, opened it at Page Two and the headline 'The House of Groome' and appeared for a few moments as if he were going to read my words for all and sundry.

Oliver J. Flanagan ordered a meal instead.

[From *The Sunday Review*, 22 July 1962. Backbencher Column]

Deputy Martin is Alive — Official

This morning I am happy to report that Deputy Martin Corry is alive and well. I have this from himself.

Last week, you'll remember, I talked about Martin's eventual successor in Dáil Éireann. Not an untimely thing considering he celebrated his Silver Jubilee in the Dáil ten years ago.

But then, Martin is no ordinary mortal. Solemnly does he assure me that he feels like a *gasúr* of 21. And, according to himself, the only concession he is willing to make to the weight of years spent on those Dáil benches is his inability to clear a five-bar gate.

But the deputy from Cork puts it so well himself. I quote: 'I did not think that I looked so bad that my early demise could be presumed. Lest, however, any of my many friends may think I am ill, or thinking of retiring, I hasten to assure them that I am in good health and if a man is as young as he feels, I am just 21, even if I can no longer clear a five-bar gate.' Gratuitously, the toothbrush-moustached representative from East Cork allows that 'both friends and enemies will admit there is nothing wrong with my tongue.'

That, if I may add my own fortuitous tuppence worth, was never in dispute — and there's no loss of his pen either. Even in his letter to me, of all people, the rugged veteran of many a Cork fight gets in a break for the commercial. I quote again: 'I can assure my constituents that whilst they require my services in the Dáil I shall always be at their disposal. Due to their kindness, I celebrated my Silver Jubilee in the Dáil 10 years ago and hope (Deo Volente) with their support to celebrate my Golden Jubilee.'

But I notice that, no more than myself, Deputy Corry appears to have his own ideas as to the man good enough to fill his Dáil boots. And fair dues to him, he hints at another proven stayer — and neatly disposes of the hopes of Seán Brosnan en route.

And who does Martin think would make a better candidate? In the best fair-ground barker manner, he ends his letter thus: '… our own East Cork star, the one and only Christy Ring'.

Martin, you're a boy!

[From *The Sunday Review*, 23 September 1962.
Backbencher Column.]

Chablis and Herrings

It isn't quite the season for Mr Teddy Lynch, the Waterford TD. The Dáil is not sitting and the Waterford Opera season is not yet at hand.

Nevertheless this does not inhibit Mr Lynch, who is currently hitting a political High C as true as the costliest star performer ever hired by the local Opera committee.

Stop him this morning on his way from Mass. He'll greet you with a chirpy salutation. Why? Because he believes he is about to be vindicated on his pet hobby-horse — and by none other than Mr Brian Lenihan of Fianna Fáil.

Galway and Killybegs he has consistently derided as the ports around which the nation's sea-fishing industry will be built. He fears not at all the danger of a herring smack across the face by Fine Gael colleagues Fintan Coogan and Pa O'Donnell.

He has, as a South-East coast man, something akin to contempt for the claims of the West and North-West, peopled as they are in his opinion by the more in-bred successors of the Fir Bolgs. But he looks to Mr Lenihan to reap him a rich harvest of votes by naming Dunmore East as the Grimsby of Ireland.

I find he has nothing but praise for Mr Lenihan. 'Dynamic' is an adjective he couples with the Roscommon man's name. For Teddy believes Brian will deliver the goods to Dunmore East. Alas, some of his adjectives for some of the other of the Fianna Fáil hierarchy are not as complimentary. Some of his friends happened to quite innocently remark that Kevin Boland had done a good job for the army. To which Teddy instantly replied: 'Yes, he's the best recruiting sergeant Her Majesty's Government ever had.'

You can pursue this line of country with him if you wish to hear a long dissertation on the failure of the language policy in the Army. I must confess I find it tiring. And what army does Mr Lynch have at heart?

Oddly, I find it is not our own. Currently he is singing the praises of the famous Fighting Sixty-Ninth. At Ballybricken, he plans to extol the great and brave deeds of Captain Patrick F. Clooney from the Irish Brigade. He boned up on their record and got more than facts: a Colour Party of the Regiment will attend a wreath-laying ceremony to be held on September 17. I can assure Mr McCloskey, the American Ambassador, that there is no need to worry about a helicopter — yet.

Teddy, of course, is the first to appreciate the political glamour of a uniform. He smiled at the news last year that Gerald Bartley, then Minister for the Gaeltacht, boosted his campaign chances not so much with Connemara Glasshouse tomatoes that never were, so much as an old photograph showing himself in an IRA uniform. Teddy, himself, had discovered the technique several years before.

The Waterford auctioneer had a patient wait in the political wings while the late Mrs Redmond held the stage. But during all that time his buttonhole was never without the regimental button from the tunic of a Redmond!

Life, however, since his arrival in Dáil Éireann, has been good to him. His auctioneering business booms. This is due to the fact that he can arouse within himself (and impart to his audience) as much enthusiasm for a commonplace farm-kitchen table as he can for a genuine Louis xiv piece. French cuisine and wine he prefers.

While the less erudite are drinking beer or stout (which he denigrates as 'bran-mash') he and colleague Sir Anthony Esmonde polish off the evening with the best Chablis the meagre cellars of Dáil Éireann have to offer. Such are their palates, and their conversations are equally choice.

Both are inveterate travellers, and can swop tales of long ago cruises, having ports of call at Genoa and Tangier.

Lynch, of course, is a Front Bench interrupter, witty at times and on occasions charmingly hurtful.

[From *The Sunday Review*, 26 August 1962.
Backbencher Column.]

15. Keeping an Eye on the Vote

So You Thought No One Knew How You Voted!

In the early 1970s, I presented a programme for RTÉ that I like to think had some tenuous connection at least, some line however thin, going back to what I first saw in my native parish in the summer of 1938.

The programme was based on local politics as operated in Donegal. The setting was very simple — two men on a Donegal hillside looking down into the valley below for as far as the eye could see. The challenge to the men was to identify the houses as they came in close-up shots on camera, to name the occupants, and then to name — on RTÉ television, a virtual monopoly channel going into nearly every house in Donegal — the party they voted for.

I had tried this programme on a number of occasions before, without success. It takes a special kind of politician(s) or activist(s), with knowledge acquired over many years to bring it off in the first place and then to have the standing and respect to gain acceptance and credibility for the judgments made. We had Tony Gallagher, a Fianna Fáil activist and for a period a member of Letterkenny UDC, and Mandy Kelly, a Fine Gael activist and an expert on agriculture. They were looking down at the houses in Meenroy Valley.

Tony: I think we're coming now to an area that will be very mixed. Mandy, you'd know some of them better than myself. ... But I think this first house here — that would be Divines —

Mandy: Fianna Fáil.

Tony: Fianna Fáil is right.

Mandy: Next one is Crossans.

Tony: They'd be Fine Gael.

Mandy: Fine Gael, that's right.

Tony: And the next ...

Mandy: The next is Gallaghers.

Tony: The Gallaghers would have been Fianna Fáil but his wife was Fine Gael and I don't know what way they voted after they got married but ... poor Mr Gallagher is dead and I hope he's happy, but I don't know what way the family are as far as politics is concerned.

Mandy: I think the family are still Fine Gael.

Tony (*laughing*): Is that right? ... The next house, John Mulhume, would be Fianna Fáil.

Mandy: Yes.

Tony: Before we move on from that house, I'd also like to quote that that's the house where my granduncle was born ... the man who wrote the very famous song 'Glenswilly'. That's the house he was born in. ... We'll have to go on up now by Meenroy.

Mandy: That's right.

Tony: And there're no other houses on the right hand side of the —

Mandy: One ... Barney McNamee's.

Tony: Oh! ... Barney McNamee, yes.

Mandy: Well, he's Fianna Fáil. Then we'll cross the

river Swilly where it rises at the foot of Meenroy to the next house, John McGinley.

Tony: John would be very —

Mandy: John's very much Fianna Fáil.

Tony: Aye … a relation of my own as well.

Mandy: We come to then …

Tony: Your own friends, Mickey McGinley.

Mandy: Mickey McGinley.

Tony: Your in-laws rather, I should have said.

Mandy: Fine Gael. And next, Fine Gael again. Move on then to the side of that mountain there, Tullyhoner. The Mulhumes are Fianna Fáil and so is Toner.

Tony: Both are Fianna Fáil.

Mandy: Yes. Move down then to the bridge.

Tony: That used to be …

Mandy: James Gallagher.

Tony: Headquarters for Fianna Fáil. They used to have their cumann meetings always there.

Mandy: That's right. It was [Neil] Blaney's head-quarters.

Tony: I think maybe it still is.

Mandy: There are two kinds of Fianna Fáil.

Tony: Aye. You're referring to the split … Blaney's Fianna Fáil and our official Fianna Fáil.

Mandy: That's right.

Tony: Oh, there are certainly two kinds of Fianna Fáil. You get a fair amount of this in this area.

Mandy: I think maybe we gained a wee bit there.

Tony: Well …

Mandy (*laughing*): We weren't as strong some time ago.

Tony: I wouldn't be as sure about that …

Mandy: We move down then to the valley here — a

little cottage in the valley here — John McDaid, he's Fine Gael.

Tony: The priest … I'm not sure.

Mandy: Well the priest …

Tony: (*laughs*)

Mandy: He tries to keep out of politics anyhow.

Tony: (*laughs*)

Mandy: Two little houses then beside us here, they're both Fianna Fáil — McDaids and McMonagles.

Tony: Oh aye, that's where Master Quinn used to live.

Mandy: That's right, Master Quinn — he was a great IRA man … at one time anyway … he's dead now.

Tony: Aye. … What would your opinion be now about the whole valley, Mandy? Take from Meenroy down to McGonagles, Rassaíodhach, that would bring in the valley.

Mandy: Well, they'd be fairly even. I'd say Fianna Fáil might have a few votes on us but …

Tony: Well, that would be my opinion.

Mandy: 'Twould only be a few votes now.

Tony: In my opinion, we'd have the majority now.

Mandy: Aye. I would say that they vote the way — the majority as far as I know them for the years down — vote the way their fathers and grandfathers and all their ancestors seemed to … well since the Troubles anyway in 1922.

Tony: But would you think mandates are not changing?

Mandy: I've known them to change. If, we'll say, a Fianna Fáil TD did something for a Fine Gael man, he might change for a year or so but … he'd be right back again and the Fianna Fáil man would be the same.

Tony: Aye, but I've got a feeling now that this last number of years back, six or seven years, people are changing for better social services and more handy money. They might not come out openly and say 'I've changed my politics. I'm going to be Fianna Fáil or I'm going to be Fine Gael.' They won't say what they're going to do, but I've a feeling when they go into the ballot box that they vote for whatever party is going to offer the most money.

I thought the two men did it beautifully, and so did Gay Byrne, who ran it twice on *The Late, Late Show*. No doubt it will make a regular appearance as RTÉ goes through its archive programmes. I only hope they will develop some system of alerting the local public when special inserts like this come up, even if only as a small section in a major programme.

Dáil Deputy Dinny McGinley who, after twenty-five years in politics, knows Donegal better than most, sees a big change in the politics of the valleys.

Changing Times
— Dinny McGinley, TD

Well you have seen there the intimate knowledge that Tony and Mandy had of the whole area around Glenswilly. You could say that the same thing was also true of most other parts of Donegal at that time: that there were political activists, mainly from Fianna Fáil and Fine Gael, who knew exactly the voting allegiances of people in their own areas. It is understandable because these were areas where there was a settled population; very few new people coming in, families there for generations and the son would take his politics from his father, who had followed his father. That's how it was.

All this has changed, not because of lack of interest in politics, but because of the changes in the countryside. There are huge developments going on in rural Ireland today: new houses being built, strangers coming in who often have no association or connection with the area; nobody knows who they are or where they're from or what affiliations they had wherever they did come from. That makes it almost impossible to have the intimate knowledge that Tony and Mandy displayed, enabling them to say with confidence how the valley voted, almost down to the last vote.

Another thing that was noticeable was that certain townlands were predominantly Fine Gael and other townlands, for some reason or another, were predominantly Fianna Fáil, and others still (like the ones Mandy and Tony were dealing with) where there was an almost equal breakdown. A lot of this really went back to the Troubles and particularly to the civil war and the sides taken by the different families.

In those times people knew almost exactly to the nearest vote what would come out of the box at the count. They always knew if there was an extra vote for someone or a vote less; they would have a really accurate picture for the next election. They spent hours going through the lists, house after house and who voted and who didn't vote and find out who changed and perhaps why! There is still an element of that in certain areas of the constituency — areas that would be rather remote, perhaps in the mountains where there have been very few new families coming in or strangers settling there, where the old families are still there. But in most of the villages now right around the coast, with new houses going up — holiday homes — we don't know who's in half of them, or where they come from. It is far more difficult to call a result now than in those days. You could say that they were able to forecast accurately not alone the seats but the votes.

But it's no longer that simple. There's a greater floating vote in rural areas. After every election the local Fianna Fáil and Fine Gael organisations — sometimes working together — used to try to account for every vote. They don't have the knowledge to do that now. They simply follow the polls on TG4. Of course there are still some experts to guide you. I can still go into areas on my canvass, and I'm sure my political opponents can do the same thing, and a local person with you will accurately point out the Fine Gael voters and the Fine Gael houses, as Fianna Fáil people are able to do too. But they are all in danger of having to give way to the housing boom.

When there's more than one candidate within your own party, then it's an entirely different story. The branch members can always tell you which members will be for your party colleague and who will be for you. That's something that we all know! We'll be told that if there's nine or ten people in a branch, there may be three of them for your political running mate and seven of them for you. Or vice versa. Where you have committed political people who are members of a branch, certainly you know the breakdown of their allegiances, whether they are for you or for your running mate. It is simple enough. That can always be worked out because you'll be told, not by the people who happen to be with your running mate, but you'll certainly be told by the people who are backing yourself. This is one thing I don't see changing.

Homebirds

The RTÉ *7 Days* programme people were doing what it liked to call an in-depth study of the way clinic and constituency work was beginning to dominate the time and the attention of Dáil deputies. It was in the early 1970s and this is when the real competition between the deputies, especially in the larger constituencies, was developing. The success of a TD was being judged by the size of the queue outside his clinics on a Saturday. If a deputy didn't want to get involved in that kind of competiton, there was always someone only too willing to help out, in the interests of the party, needless to say.

We decided that a convenient place to record some of the interviews with Fine Gael people would be at the party's ard-fheis. We lined up about fifteen in all — Dáil deputies, councillors and party activists — in an informal setting in one of the bars. As a presenter of the programme, I was talking to Maurice Dockrell (Dublin South-Central).

'I suppose that with the present concentration on clinic work, Deputy, you have to spend a lot of your time in the Liberties area?' I started.

'Where are the Liberties?' came the booming reply from Maurice, and with it the collapse of our recording in laughter.

You see, not only had Maurice been deputy for Dublin South-Central since 1948 (and for Dublin South 1943–48), the extensive family business of H.P. Dockrell was also based in that general area, and one out of every three or four CIÉ buses passing through would be carrying a Dockrell advertisement.

Another survey we did around the same time was on the importance TDs attached to living in their own constituencies to 'guard' their seats. The figures speak for themselves.

In the mid-1970s the Dáil had 144 deputies, and of these 110 lived in their own constituencies, a further twenty-three lived in close proximity (say two miles in rural constituencies), a further three deputies within ten miles (one of these found himself outside rather than inside the tent after a constituency revision). Of the remaining eight, six had residences, but not principal residences, in their constituencies. The remainder was accounted for by former ministers, who had moved to Dublin many years earlier, when Fianna Fáil was the permanent government of the country.

It was ironic then that the question of residency in the constituency was the first challenge I had to face when I sought a nomination from the Fine Gael convention in Sligo–Leitrim to become a candidate for the party in the 1981 general election. I was being 'parachuted in' was the accusation. In an election campaign, that was fair enough. I had been away from Sligo for thirty years and had no place of residence there. It was my bad luck that the constituency already had for years one non-resident deputy, elected from the south of the area. He was a Fianna Fáil man. But that minor matter did not inhibit them since they warned that I would do the same — become an absentee TD. Criticism was a bit diffuse at first until Councillor Willie Farrell, Chairman of Sligo County Council, got involved. Willie is very good at this kind of thing, and regularly made the headlines in *The Sligo Champion*. He's the man who once told Sligo Planning Committee that its members were so rigid and so lacking in imagination that if Queen Maeve came along looking for planning permission for a cairn on the top of her grave on Knocknarea, one of the great landmarks of the West, they'd refuse.

One of his colleagues told me that Willie often thought up his best lines as he drove from his home in Grange, County Sligo, to the various meetings he had to attend. This evening he was going to Collooney, to the Fianna Fáil nomination convention for the general election candidates. Wherever the inspiration came from, maybe the B&B advertising signs, Willie landed a direct hit on my campaign when he christened me the 'Bed and Breakfast TD'. It was the perfect campaign one-liner for the canvassers. They gave Willie an ovation at the convention.

There are some times when it's best, even in party politics, to acknowledge a hit and move on. But when Willie was elected to a Senate that collapsed almost immediately I couldn't resist. I apologised for not being able to refer to him as the 'Bed and Breakfast Senator'. He didn't have time to wait for his breakfast!

Career Changes

In the 1960s I moved from newspapers, where I had become editor of the *Sunday Review*, to a job on RTÉ's farming programmes. It was a hopeful time for agriculture in Ireland. The country was being prepared: the jackets were off. But my particular area of interest was politics, and in due course I became a political commentator on the hard-hitting, parameter pushing *7 Days* programme, which, much like *The Late, Late Show* today, saw people adjusting their social activities on Tuesday and Thursday nights to see 'what row would the lads have tonight'. If a programme was bad, they didn't blame the makers, they blamed events; that's when you know a current affairs programme has made it. In the 1973 general election I had a bit of a bonus myself, being credited with beating the computer and everyone else, in predicting the final outcome of seats. I also won the RTÉ general election sweepstakes!

Next morning, Professor Basil Chubb of the Political Science department in Trinity College arrived with a full colour graphic of my progress. The caption read, 'It's 18.48, Nealon predicts 68 for Fianna Fáil on air.' The result was 69. The best — and indeed the most cynical — comment I remember came from Bill O'Herlihy who was in current affairs with *7 Days* at the time: 'Good show, Ted. You needn't do another bat of work for the next four years, until the next election.'

Much to my surprise I was contacted by Conor Cruise O'Brien, then Minister for Posts and Telegraphs, on behalf of the government of Liam Cosgrave and Brendan Cornish. He offered me the job of head of the Government Information Services or, as it is now called, press secretary to the Taoiseach.

I went to New York with my wife for a week's holidays, leaving no forwarding address. On Sunday morning, Joe Malone of the Irish Tourist Board was given the task by the government of locating me in New York. He decided to call every Nealon listed in the telephone directory! Eventually he came to a cousin of mine, Mike Nealon.

'We're trying to trace a Ted Nealon and rang in the hope that he might be with you.'

'No, he's not here now but I'm expecting him for 2 o'clock lunch and the man has a big appetite — he'll be here.'

I was back in New York again for the bicentennial celebrations, in my new role as press secretary to the Taoiseach Liam Cosgrave. It was the turn of the Irish to throw the last party of the tour, which they did in style with the Taoiseach as host. The location was the Waldorf Astoria. I had one special guest, my ninety-two-year-old aunt Katherine, who had left Ireland more than fifty years earlier and never returned. She'd brought up a large and talented family in Staten Island but because of the war she'd missed out on ever coming home.

I introduced her to Mr Cosgrave and asked if she was proud to be meeting the Taoiseach, remembering the way things were when she'd left Ireland. With a Coolrecull blas as unchanged as if she'd never gone further than neighbour Lundy's well, and with no disrespect to her host intended, she replied, 'Sure it's you I came here to see, Ted, not Mr Cosgrave.'

16. Among the Grassroots

Representatives from Clare

Because of the dominance of the Fianna Fáil party in a popular vote, Clare constituency has never attracted the same close analysis as the marginals constantly do. In the 1973 general election, the Fianna Fáil vote in Clare was sixty-two per cent, the only constituency to give over sixty per cent of its votes to any one party in any part of the country. Despite the passing from the scene of Éamon de Valera, the radical change in attitudes in rural Ireland and the weakening of the inherited politics of the 'gene pools', Clare is still a Fianna Fáil stronghold and many would say will continue to be for some years to come.

What will be more difficult to maintain will be the extraordinary blend of representatives that general elections produced there down the years — as befitted the constituency that had Daniel O'Connell as a Member of Parliament in the House of Commons.

Foremost of all there was Éamon de Valera, elected for Clare for forty-two years, 1917–59, and then becoming Úachtarán na hÉireann. For his constituents, he was, of necessity, a rather remote man, generally away running the country or — very occasionally — the Opposition. When the faithful followers came to see him at Carmody's Hotel, they were there more to pay homage to the Chief than for any other purpose, and while he couldn't be with them like other Dáil deputies, things would be well looked after. And, of course, there was always a presence at the Ennis Show.

After the 1951 election, de Valera was joined as a Dáil deputy by a young medical doctor, Patrick Hillery, another man destined to become Úachtarán na hÉireann. In the following years the sage and the acolyte could be seen regularly in consultation, presumably on constituency affairs, in the lobby of the Dáil, while votes were in progress. Dr Hillery practised as a GP in his native Spanish Point and also ran constituency clinics in the area. When I was working for RTÉ on a *7 Days* biopic programme on Dr Hillery, he allowed me to film his political clinic. For a bit of fun, I asked one of the callers if there wasn't a danger of a mix-up arising between clients for the medical and those for the political clinic.

'No danger at all of such a mix-up with Dr Paddy,' he replied. 'He knows by the look of you the moment you arrive what kind of attention you need. And I'll tell you something else, Mr Nealon, something that you boys in Dublin mightn't understand: he could probably also tell you which way every one of the callers vote. But that's a subject that never comes up.'

Dr Hillery was Minister in the Departments of Foreign Affairs, Labour, and Education, and as Minister for Foreign Affairs headed the Irish government's negotiations for joining the European Economic Community. He was Ireland's first Commissioner.

Dr Hillery was a leading golfer and took part in many of the major competitions. He was also very interested in landscape painting and I myself had the privilege of doing a course with him one winter, under the guidance of Henry Healy, President of the Royal Hibernian Academy, in an attic studio in Francis Street, Dublin, before the transformation of that area. The studio was adequate but the approach stairs were not the kind you would expect to see Úachtarán na hÉireann using. They suffered from a deficit of timber.

———

In the late 1930s and early 1940s, politics in Ireland was beginning to sprout, with four elections in five years and the arrival on the scene of a new political party, the Clare Farmers Party, chasing a seat in Dev's own constituency, no less.

The Clare Farmers Party, to be followed later by Clann na Talmhain and Clann na Poblachta, seemed to be well organised and to be pretty good at promoting themselves. The sense of injustice and neglect felt by the farmers at that time would ensure a good vote anyhow (as it did for Clann na Talmhain later on). What the Clare Farmers Party lacked, as did many a party before and since, was a 'front man' who would be, for whatever reason, credible to the electorate. When they looked, they couldn't find any such person amongst their own ranks. So they decided to adopt one — a bone-setter called Thomas Burke, a man of great renown for the work he was doing throughout the county, or what they would call in later years, a man of great charisma.

At that time in Ireland, bonesetting was guided by a number of very strong traditions. First of all it had to be inherited, not acquired in any other way. Another strong tradition was that the bonesetter must not accept payment for his work. Burke belonged to a family of bonesetters and gave his full time to it. He was already a member of Clare County Council and 'was thinking' of running for the Dáil election in 1937. The Clare Farmers Party decided that here was the answer — this was the man they would adopt — so they sent a delegation to Ennis where the bonesetter was holding a clinic. With the affinity of interests, the talks did not take too long. There was only one hitch — not really a hitch, but a short adjournment — while Burke fixed the dislocated ankle of one of the delegates.

With the right name for the posters, the party was in business and it bought space in *The Clare Champion*, stressing Burke's personality and renown:

> Tommy Burke, as he is familiarly called, is worthy of support on humanitarian grounds. Now is the time for those whose sufferings he has alleviated to show their gratitude. He has gone to your homes at all hours of the day and night when you needed him and his fee was a handshake … the candidate who doesn't make empty promises and is humanity's best friend.

Burke came second in the first preference votes behind de Valera and took the fourth seat of five. While the new Dáil deputy continued to work as a bonesetter, he didn't consider it amongst his priorities to attend election counts or party meetings or to make speeches.

The chairman of the Clare Farmers Party told an AGM that 'some might describe their representative as a question mark or say he did not represent anybody'. Otherwise, the chairman's speech was supportive. The prospect of another election restored party harmony again and the public relations this time had even got an election song:

> The day at last is dawning
> When the Farmers, tired of yawning,
> Will sally forth now gallantly and say
> With one loud ringing voice:
> THOMAS BURKE will get our choice
> We'll give HIM No. 1 on polling day.
>
> Now remember THOMAS BURKE.
> Don't forget his noble work;

His county, and outside it, can proclaim.
That the bone his hand will touch,
It will never need a crutch,
For his county he will ever do the same.

So Clare Farmers one and all
With your wives both big and small
And your children who have come to Twenty-One,
While the sweat is on your brow
Won't you make this solemn vow
To reward him for the good that he has done.

Burke came third in the poll. He actually made an appearance at the count and, even more unusually, gave a speech. It was to deny the allegations made, according to Burke, that he had refused his services as a bonesetter to supporters of political opponents.

When the 1948 election was called, the chances of Thomas Burke retaining his seat were predicted to be poor to practically non-existent. This belief was shared, surprisingly, by himself. So he felt something drastic was needed to turn around his fortunes. As usual, he bought space in *The Clare Champion* but not, as expected, to woo the electorate, to seek to recover the votes he felt he was losing or even to attack the other candidates on the ballot paper. His targets were the voters themselves. He berated them; he accused them of ingratitude. He told them that for years he had helped them without reward and now they were about to cost him his seat! Why did he have to beg them? All this in a paid-for advertisement!

This approach is one I haven't heard of before and I don't think it has been practised since the days of the bonesetter from Clare. But it worked! He took the third seat with very good transfers. The next election in 1951 was just that bit too much for his endurance. He lost the fifth seat to the Labour candidate by just over a hundred votes, despite getting eighty-nine per cent of Patrick Hillery's surplus.

As always with Thomas Burke, there was a scattering of messages left for him when the ballot boxes were being emptied out. The last ones included the following:

> Here's one for Tom Burke, the Bonesetter,
> When the missus fell over her sweater,
> He patched up her bones
> And silenced her groans
> Whether that was for worse or for better.

Thomas Burke died on 20 November 1951, only five months after losing his seat. In a tribute, *The Clare Champion* said: 'His forty years as a councillor and fourteen years as a TD are a fitting tribute to his skills as a bonesetter and a lasting indication of the gratitude and esteem in which he was held by the people of County Clare.'

_____

Another distinguished representative from Clare was Patrick Hogan (Labour), Ceann Comhairle for sixteen years from 1951 to 1967, better known nowadays for the fact that he wrote 'The Shawl of Galway Grey'.

Waders
During the first FitzGerald short-lived government (June 1981–March 1982) I was Minister of State for Western development. The instant Garret made the official announcement, my phone rang at Leinster House. It was Malachy Canning of Feenagh, County Leitrim. He ignored the niceties.

'Will you have "the car" home with you tomorrow?' he asked me, and anyone who knew Malachy knew that 'the car' he was talking about was the ministerial Mercedes that went with the job at the time. For him it was in permanent quotation marks!

Malachy was a Fine Gael worker all his life. If you wanted him as chairman of the constituency organisation, sure that was alright. If you wanted him to take up a collection, it was the same thing. And he was typical of the volunteer workers who enable Fine Gael — and the same goes for the other parties — to have an organisation. I feel that there is a very important layer of people in politics, like Malachy, who never get the recognition and respect for the work they do for democracy.

'With all due respect to yourself, Minister, what the people down here want to see is not you but "the car". I'm talking about the people who went out and did the work, put up the posters, called on the houses and, more often than not, let's be honest, ended up without anything to shout about. This time we do have something to shout about, and "the car" is the nearest we'll get to a symbol of the handover, that the bragging rights are now with us. We'll call a meeting,' he said, 'and I'll leave plenty of parking space for you in front of the hall, enough to do the whole cabinet if you could get them to come down.'

Malachy himself presided at the meeting. As a Leitrim man, he would have voted his first preference for the Leitrim candidate, but in his speech of welcome to the new Minister he certainly did me proud. I would finish off the arterial drainage of the River Bonet, waiting its turn to be done since the 1940s. I had direct charge of the budget line for land drainage. He was only getting into his stride when someone from the crowd decided to get involved for a bit of fun.

'What exactly does our Minister for Western Development do? Does he run the whole West of Ireland?'

Malachy replied: 'Leitrim for the time being, and when he's finished with that — and if we're still in power — he might tackle the rest.'

'Would I be right in saying that he more or less holds the same job that Percy French did when he worked a few miles away across the border in County Cavan as His Majesty's Inspector of Drains?'

'Something the same, except that poor old Percy had to get round on his bicycle and the Minister has "the car",' said Malachy.

The only time the meeting got down to business of sorts was when a motion was passed demanding that the Minister, within a week, inspect the work on the Bonet. This seemed to me to be designed as another outing for 'the car'.

The first halt of the Bonet tour was in Dromahair, to pick up Councillor John McTiernan.

'Thanks for coming, Minister. You're looking well but you're not properly attired for the job in hand,' he said as he joined me in the car. 'You know, Minister, what you called the floods at the last protest meeting you attended in the Ballroom of Romance in Glenfarne, when we weren't burdened with the responsibility of office. You called them the worst floods since Noah had to put sandbags on the Ark! Now your shoes — suede — are not the footwear for floods like that! "The car" may be all they're saying but it cannot float.'

John McTiernan also gently reminded me that we had something of a record in the Sligo–Leitrim constituency where the left foot didn't always know what the right foot was doing. So we headed off to Kilasnett Creamery.

While I knew from party meetings just how serious the people in the catchment area were about having the Bonet drainage completed, I soon found out that on this day, lining up in convoy behind 'the car' was more than half the fun.

'That's a rare bird indeed in these parts, a ministerial Mercedes car under a local Fine Gael TD!' said a man from Manorhamilton. Before attracting much attention for my brown suede shoes, I hurried into the shop of the local Creamery Co-op where, hanging from the roof, was the finest collection of waders and wellingtons I have ever seen, in colours of black and green.

'Welcome to Kilasnett, Minister,' said the manager. 'Can I help you?'

'What I want are waders or wellingtons, but I can't quite make up my mind which to go for. I have no doubt they're both of excellent quality.'

'Can I ask you what you want them for?'

'Well, right now, as you see, I want them for the inspection of the Bonet flooding.'

'Well, it's the waders you're looking for. It's the waders. What size do you take, Minister?'

There's Still Hope

After the general election of 1948, there was no absolute certainty of who would be the next Taoiseach, Éamon de Valera again or John A. Costello for the first time. Mr de Valera had been Taoiseach continuously since 1932. After the election he had sixty-eight seats (including the outgoing Ceann Comhairle), so, despite the strength of the smaller parties and of the Independents, it looked as if there would be a change of government. However, Fianna Fáil was not inclined to concede.

Patrick J. Lindsay, then a practising lawyer on the Western Circuit, was, no doubt, happy with the eventual outcome. First of all, he didn't have to worry about parking his car! Pat Lindsay has this story to tell in his memoir, *Memories*.

Patrick Lindsay

I have however one great memory of that 1948 election, or rather of its aftermath. There was no certainty that an Inter-Party Government could be put together or that de Valera could be ousted — indeed most Fianna Fáil people refused to even contemplate such a thing happening, including I believe de Valera himself. In any event, the heavy speculation continued right up to the last minute.

I was out of Dublin, frustratingly out of touch on circuit in Galway, on the day the new Dáil met. I waited as long as I could in Galway to get the result of the election for Taoiseach, but I had to go to Dunmore for a consultation with a solicitor there, Ambrose Nestor.

I was going down the road to Tuam when I saw papal flags flying out of some houses and I said to myself, 'He's back again,' the 'he' being de Valera. Then I continued on my journey and I met a fellow on a bicycle with his cap turned backways. He looked to me like a typical Fianna Fáil road ganger and he looked vicious and disappointed, and I thought, 'There's still hope.'

I drove into Tuam and I saw there the large physique of a man, a civic guard, who was standing on the footpath. I pulled in diagonally and lowered my window.

'Guard, is there any news from Dublin?'

'At ten past five this afternoon, John Aloysius Costello was elected Taoiseach of the Country.'

I knew by the way he said it that this really meant something to him, and I said:

'Guard, would you like a drink?'

'We'll have two.'

'Will you wait a minute until I park this car?'

'Leave it where it is. We have freedom for the first time in sixteen years.' We had more than one drink that day.

[Patrick Lindsay, *Memories*, Blackwater Press, 1992]

The ineffable Pat Lindsay composed his own postscript to the multitude of anecdotes relating to his colourful life. During his final illness, he accepted an invitation from some of his greatest admirers to attend a 'going away' party at the home of his close friend Maurice Manning.

Accompanied by a nurse, he arrived straight from his hospital bed to a rapturous reception, and with a large whiskey in one hand and his trademark cigar in the other, delivered an unforgettably witty speech without a trace of self-pity.

He concluded: 'I got a phone call from Joe Cassidy [the Bishop of Clonfert] this morning. Sez he: "Pat, it comes to us all, but I can tell you this, your sins are forgiven." I could only reply: "Well, thank you, Joe, and I'll tell you this. My only regret is that I didn't commit more of them while I was able!"'

Within days the lion-hearted Lindsay had passed away.

Clinic for a Poitín Distiller

For the poitín-maker, or illicit distiller as he is known to the courts, a guilty verdict is now a costly business. The average penalty can be a fine of €1,000, or, in default, six months in prison. In fairness, it has to be said that the gardaí, who are the people who initiate the proceedings, are never in too much of a hurry to collect the fine. At some stage, however, a move must be made and this is usually where politicians become involved. Generally it starts with a request from the poitín-maker to one or more local TD to make representations on his behalf for a mitigation of the fine on compassionate grounds. This is something of a 'shot to nothing' because if there is no mitigation of the court penalty granted, the processing is always a long-drawn-out procedure, giving the applicant in the meantime the equivalent of an interest-free loan.

Poitín cases do not figure very much any more in a Dáil deputy's clinic, even in the western constituencies. During the year before I retired from the Dáil in 1997, I had one poitín case. The man, a good supporter of my own at the ballot box, or so he said, came from the north-east of my Sligo–Leitrim constituency or, as he put it himself, 'from the territory where the Breffni chiefs once ruled and made their own poitín'. He asked me to call to his house. From the start this was not going to be a routine Saturday clinic where getting around to all advertised locations without falling too far behind schedule is a key objective — what the deputy on the clinic trail would call 'establishing a presence'.

'I'd like to review things with you,' my client had told me on the phone. I knew from experience that his 'review' could range from saving Gaelic football in Sligo to saving the world. Since he lived on his own, with his next-door neighbour a mile away down a pot-holed forest road, he was always anxious for a chat. Then there was the serious matter of his unpaid court fine for illicit distillation. It was getting near the time when he would have to pay up or pack his bags for jail. He had made no mention of representations about the fine. The first thing I asked him was how a man of his lifetime experience, revered in the poitín business, operating on the commonage in the foothills of his own mountains, could get caught so simply.

'How did I get caught so simply? The answer is the silly way, the silly way. After all the years of warning my fellow distillers, when in production, never to touch a drop of the new stuff, never to put a mug to your lips until all the evidence of recent activity is hidden and where necessary buried away, to leave your house looking as innocent as if you were having the Stations the next day or expecting the parish priest, maybe the only priest to call to have a look at you for the Last Rites, but I didn't follow my own advice. I did the silly thing. I broke my own rules and when I woke up there were three Guards in the place — one outside feeding the dog, one in the kitchen watching an old video of Manchester United when they used to win something, and the third one watching me. With the way I was, I couldn't make a bolt for it even if I got a hundred yards' start on the Sergeant, who himself was ready to retire when the pension was right. Three Guards in a house up on the side of the mountain! I was running a poitín still, not a riot.

'I pleaded guilty straight away. It may be that I'm not as sharp as I used to be, but at the time I couldn't think of any other options. Anyway, I'm finished with the poitín-making. It was a bit sad vacating my pitch in an area where I could recognise one hare from another as they skipped by, and where I knew I was shielded by the heather-covered bogholes from any danger of physical pursuit by the law. I have decided that it's no longer a job for me. I did my share to preserve the standards.'

Then I asked him if there were many like him who had packed it in.

'Most of what I would call the class operators, the professional poitín-for-cash men whose produce you could always rely on, have retired, hidden away their equipment and it won't be taken back. These men were generally small farmers and for them it was a bit of off-farm activity when the nights got longer. They needed the money. We were a by-product of our times, not people who liked to break the law, as we are often portrayed.

'Mark Clinton was the man who finished poitín-making in the west of Ireland. I know what you're going to say, that Mark Clinton was Minister for Agriculture and had nothing to do with poitín, that I'm mixing ministers. Then I'm afraid, Deputy, you're not getting my drift.

'Mark Clinton did it with the grants that he got for the small farmers from Europe when he walked out of that meeting in Brussels in the early 70s. The cheques in the post were steadier than the cheques from the poitín. Who did you want knocking on the door — the postman or the policeman? I'm told that when a child is born in Dubai, the first thing it gets is a pension! Well we never got that here but when the headage grants and the hedges grants and the grants for everything else came from Europe, we were nearly as good as the best of them. There was a grant one time for putting more sheep up the mountain, and then when that didn't work out and bald patches began to show with the over-grazing, there were new grants for putting the sheep down again. I used to call it "The Grand Old Duke of

York money". The real core of the poitín industry was the small farmer from the mountainside. He had the suitable terrain and needed the bit of extra cash. When Europe provided the cash flow, a lot got out of poitín, which proves, I suppose, that they didn't really want to be in it in the first place.

'There was always during my lifetime a share of confused thinking about poitín. Even the Catholic Church was not too clear in its stance. In one diocese not far from here, it was a reserved sin to drink poitín, never mind to make it. How could it be a reserved sin, with absolution only from the Bishop, in one diocese, and a "Here's to your good health" down the road? It used to be said that the profits from the poitín in the past put many a good man through Maynooth!

'There was also the role of poitín as an "alternative" medicine. Many families liked to have the comfort of a few bottles for the winter period hidden in a haycock or a stack of oats. It was supposed to be great for preventing 'flu and, even better, for a cure if you got the 'flu. I saw a few men in my time calling here in the middle of the week for a bottle whom you'd swear were on their last legs. The following Sunday they'd be out at first Mass before you. Young Guards of today don't seem to appreciate this particular tradition as much as some of the older men. They'll tell you, if you don't mind, you'd be better off getting the 'flu injection! Anyhow, we no longer have the haycocks or the stacks of oats. You wouldn't fancy hiding poitín in one of those round bales wrapped in black plastic.

'So for all this combination of reasons, poitín-making is gone or is well on the way. But it was part of our tradition, part of our heritage, and it's necessary that we do something to keep the actual skills; otherwise, they'll be gone as soon as the people who made the poitín and who drank it are gone. Things decay very quickly if they aren't used. I'm sure you'd be hard put to it to find a man in the County Sligo now who would make you a decent pair of *partógs*.

'I may not be the best man to say it, but we need some sort of a poitín centre, making the real stuff and not some sort of pretend stuff. I once heard Peter Barry, the Cork minister, describing himself as a tea taster by profession. That's a job I could do myself for a poitín centre. Quality is everything. Maybe you'd put in a good word for me somewhere. And you needn't bother making any representations on the other matter for me. We'll let the hare sit. I just wanted, in some way, to mark my retirement without putting myself in jeopardy again. I'm sorry I can't offer you a drink. There's nothing in the house.'

Forgetting Names

Ideally, a good memory for names and faces is something every practising politician should have. There are no dividends in chasing up a constituency problem for six months, having your secretary send out 'Dear Tom' letters reporting progress and then not recognising the person in question when you accidentally run into him in town. That's why you will scarcely ever hear a Dáil deputy, in his own territory at least, saying 'I'm sorry but your name escapes me for the moment.'

When I was elected to the Dáil in 1981, I had major difficulties with names. By way of an excuse, I would explain to party members that I had been away from Sligo–Leitrim for thirty-five years and had no bedrock bank of names to start with. They weren't impressed, but then it's not always easy to impress party members.

A canny Cork colleague, with a deserved reputation for being good at these kind of things, offered to give me a bit of advice and help, never suggesting, of course, that he had heard that I needed it rather badly.

The first bit of advice is that when you are approached by a constituent, you give the impression that you know whom you are talking to, or at the very least leave him or her confused about your state of knowledge. In other words, you bluff. After all, you don't want people going around saying, 'This man we sent to Leinster House doesn't recognise anyone.' That's the kind of stray talk that spreads like a bog fire in the early spring.

What you do next is throw out a simple question like 'How are things out your way?' You cannot get much vaguer than that but, believe me, that's the kind of probe that brings the clues. Maybe your constituent will say that he is going to a big wedding at a local church the next day or, as happened to me recently, that a neighbour of his own and a supporter of mine was rushed off to hospital in an ambulance. Nothing serious, thank God. After that, with any sort of well-judged supplementary, you have the exact location where your constituent lives. You still haven't got the name, of course, but one phone call the next morning should do that for you.

You then start to repair any possible damage that your forgetting the name might have done. I usually do this by way of a 'Dear Peter' letter, saying how delighted I was to meet him in the town; that he looks so well he's going from knowing. I would then thank him for letting me know about his neighbour being in hospital and that I had sent her a 'Get Well' card, mentioning of course that it was from himself that I got the news.

Sometimes, depending on my humour, I'd also organise a message of congratulations to the wedding party. With a bit of luck, and a bit of wit in the telegram, these can sometimes be read out. Peter would be there listening and wondering.

On your walk-abouts, you can also run into another type of constituent, a good worker at election time but in between elections the kind of man you think would prefer to embarrass you than praise you. He'll half-introduce himself, like 'I'm one of the Kellys from Riverside.' The answer for that is 'I know you're one of the Kellys from Riverside, but what won't come to my mind at the moment is your first name.'

Not that I don't still get caught out with the odd name myself. Only last week I met with a real old stalwart of the party, a very familiar face, but I just couldn't bring his name to the surface. This man probably has a Fine Gael long service certificate hanging in his hallway. Maybe he had been in the Blue Shirts. But the name wouldn't come to me. I wasn't long home from town when I found out. Another old party supporter rang up.

'You were talking to Tommy Healy in town I heard.'

'Yes, how did you know?'

'He just phoned me up himself. He wants you to do a little job for him.'

'Why didn't he ask me himself?'

'Well, to be blunt, he knew that after all those years you still couldn't come up with his name when he met you in town like that. He didn't want to embarrass you, so he asked me to pass along the details to you. Decent man, Tommy!'

Máire

Máire was accepted by all as the best party worker in the constituency, and you could throw in a few of the neighbouring constituencies as well. She was tough when things didn't go right — that is, when things didn't go her way. And all the indicators were that she appeared to be moving into a hostile position as far as the Dáil deputy was concerned.

'There's a man who's got awful full of himself since the last election, our esteemed TD,' she shouted to her husband when she returned from shopping, even before she had put away the groceries. 'I met him down past the crossroads and gave him a big jolly wave. But he just drove on as if I didn't exist. How can you be enthusiastic about a man like that? And there's another thing, what was he doing down here anyway? I suppose for tactical talks with our new chairman, or to use the words of Mark Durkan [leader of the SDLP], to orchestrate their u-turns. If he tries any fancy u-turns around here, he'll find himself ending up on the hard shoulder.'

At this stage one of the party activists, called James, dropped in for a sort of an *ad limina* visit to Máire, as was the custom with a lot of the activists. He joined in the conversation: 'There is always a bit of a problem about waving for our Dáil deputy or any other Dáil deputy, so don't be too hard on him. There is no way any longer, even in rural areas, where a deputy could know all the cars as they used to and much less of a chance of recognising in the distance the driver, without the car, so to speak.'

'And why not?' asked Máire. 'What else does our man use his head for, except as a storage compartment for names to impress with his so-called local knowledge? All he's worried about, in his own words, is "image". No bloody work.'

James persisted, in spite of the danger of bringing real fire from Máire.

'It's difficult to keep everyone happy, so what I see most of the TDs doing is, once driving in their own constituency, saluting every car, and getting out of it that way. But it's not always the solution either.'

'Why not?' asked Máire. 'Is it too much to expect your Dáil deputy to salute nowadays, too demanding on the poor man?'

'It's not the effort at all that I'm talking about. It's the way a salute can be misunderstood,' said James. 'Supposing the TD doing the waving is Fine Gael and the driver in the oncoming car is a Fianna Fáil activist, what's his reaction going to be? Is it going to be "That cheeky bastard" or is it going to be "Why has your man got so friendly all of a sudden?" There is the danger of what's known these days, Máire, as negative fall-out!'

'Very smart you're all getting. So what's the solution if you're that good?' snapped Máire.

Máire's husband joined in the conversation and what he had to say usually made a lot of sense.

'Well, we had a TD in this area once who worked out his own answer to the problem, but it involved a bit of a change in his driving style. The first two fingers he never removed from the steering wheel. The other two were constantly pointed in a heavenwards direction. Each time a car came towards him he rolled the fingers that little bit farther heavenwards. That was his salute. He found that those of his own party took it as a friendly wave and were appreciative of it. His political opponents took a totally different view of his salute. As far as they were concerned, he was going back to basics.

'These are all only minor problems,' James said. 'What about the problems of the man from Laois–Offaly, who, a long time ago now, bought the old car that Oliver J. Flanagan had traded in? For the next two or three years they were still saluting the car, much to the amusement of the old and the new owners. Oliver at one stage even suggested that the new owner might run for the Council!'

The Almighty Man

Prayers and politics do sometimes mix, although one thing you're unlikely to see at election time is a Dáil candidate coming down your street with his canvass team, arriving at your door and asking for your prayers. The first and basic reason is that once an election is called, candidates can think of one thing only: votes and initially first preference votes. They all subscribe to Oliver J. Flanagan's principle that 'there is no such thing as too many No. 1 votes'.

The second reason is that a candidate, whatever his belief in the power of prayer, cannot let the word go out that he was canvassing for prayers on the doorsteps. It would be already back in the pub that evening before him, probably with a few bars added:

'I hear that you are conceding already?' he'd be told.

'Not even asking for the votes; it can't be that bad.'

But prayer for election success has always been a strong traditional practice, certainly in the Sligo–Leitrim constituency. Voters who may be strangers approach candidates on the street to wish them good luck and tell them that they'll be praying for them or calling on their favourite saint to intercede — the same as they do if someone is ill. Candidates are regularly told they'll be alright 'with the help of God'.

A message like that is always encouraging for the candidate, even in what's called a safe seat (there's no such thing as a safe seat). But then in such circumstances should the candidate further press on for a commitment of the vote or should he assume that the votes will follow the prayers? The attitude of my canvassers, by no means the most aggressive in the field, was that you assume nothing, that you press on for an absolute commitment and, while you are at it, you may as well go for the No.1 vote. Pakie McGowan, our star canvasser, always thought that this was a good opportunity to try to get a few No.1s for the weaker candidate to keep them in the race as long as possible. An early elimination often ruins transfer tactics and vote management.

In the general election of 1992, the Spring tide election, there were only a few days to go before voting by the time we got out to canvass a couple of parishes in Tireragh. The first house we canvassed was that of a man we'll name Tony. At every election I fought — and they were coming pretty frequently in the 1980s — Tony had always responded in precisely the same way. 'Your seat will be alright with the help of the Almighty,' he would tell me, 'and you'll have my vote again, but as I explained to you previously, it has nothing to do with party allegiances. It's because of our friendship when we were playing under-age football together.' Not surprisingly, he was referred to by our canvassers from outside the area as 'the Almighty man'.

But despite his regular reference to reliance on the Almighty, Tony was a man who kept himself very well informed on political matters and on what was happening at the grass-roots.

On our canvass in 1992 the talk everywhere was of the progress being made by the Labour Party and of the extent of the Spring tide. All the surveys were showing that Labour, for the first time since the foundation of the State, would elect a TD for Sligo–Leitrim. They had a good candidate in Alderman Declan Bree, although he had been defeated many times previously.

If Labour were to win a seat, then the seat at most risk would be the Fine Gael seat where I was the outgoing deputy, that is if the votes went where they were supposed to go when the constituency was divided up for vote management.

'What advice have you for me before I go ?' I asked Tony.

'As I said to you before, you'll hold on with the help of the Almighty, but with all due respect and no offence meant to anyone, it seems to me some votes are slipping. I know three people that you did a very good turn for and they won't be voting for you this time and they were Fine Gael by birth. And there's a man across the fields — rural Ireland, good rural Ireland at that — and do you know that he has a Labour poster in his window, although I admit that it also helps to keep out the draught. I asked him why the change and do you know what he told me: a niece in Dublin had given him a book on great Labour leaders, including Jim Larkin, and he was greatly influenced by that man.'

'So, Tony, what do you suggest I should be doing, changing to Plan B?'

'If you have a Plan B ... sure even an Irish football coach would have moved to Plan B by now. But your Plan B must do a number of things.'

'Like what?'

'If you have a Plan B and it contains what I think it should contain, do it. Calling in every Fine Gael vote capable of being moved; go into the areas you're not supposed to be in; you should be sleeping in forbidden areas. You should be already turning your car. The job you're in was never meant to be a career option for good losers!'

'What would the Almighty do?'

'I know the allusions you are making, but I don't know the

answer. You see, Deputy, the Almighty hasn't come up against anything like the Spring tide before!'

Clans

During the 1960s, Radio Éireann, as it was then known, had a very popular Sunday show called *Meet the Clans*. Essentially it was an 'ask the expert' style of programme on all matters genealogical, with the queries sent in by postcard or letter. There was no hint of controversy, manufactured or otherwise. But it worked.

It worked because of the phenomenal knowledge in this field of the chief anchorman and main presenter, Eoin O'Mahony, 'The Pope' as he was known to everyone.

The information, unscripted, was delivered by him at a furious pace, with asides and embellishments as he went along. He left the listeners with the impression that he was talking of people known to him personally, or that he was on first name terms with them, if a title didn't get in the way. (Indeed, long before *Meet the Clans* the door was on the latch for The Pope, with an invitation to stay for as long as he wished in houses all over the country, big and small. He frequently availed of these invitations, more or less permanently moving around the country.)

Although a barrister and Queen's Counsel, he didn't practise in either jurisdiction, except once for a famous defence of a young Brendan Behan. During the course of his pleadings to that court, The Pope described Behan as 'a love child of the Revolution'. Behan was sent to Borstal.

The Pope's name came up regularly as a potential candidate in general elections and indeed in many of the by-elections. On one occasion he threw his very distinctive hat in the ring in his native Cork, getting a Fianna Fáil nomination in Cork Central. He got off to a flying start, with no need for introductions. Everyone knew The Pope anyhow. And he attracted large crowds when he 'did Panna'. Someone remarked, maybe himself, that he had a quota of the curious anyhow, whatever about a quota in the ballot box. As was anticipated, the parachuting of The Pope into the constituency, although it was his native Cork, was not greeted with bonfires or welcome by the outgoing Dáil deputies and candidates, including, or probably especially, from his own party.

The boundaries of Cork Central constituency had recently been revised. This would normally not be to the disadvantage of a high-profile candidate coming on the scene for the first time. However, it proved the undoing of The Pope's campaign to get Leinster House added to his list of open doors. With the revision of the constituency boundary comes a revision of the voting register. Unfortunately, the old register was mistakenly used at the beginning of The Pope's campaign. In other words, his flying start and good response were for real but the voters were not for real. He was canvassing the wrong people.

Sadly for Eoin O'Mahony, the Lee tide never came in.

17. A Question of Heritage

The Blaskets

The Blasket Island Foundation (Fondreacht an Bhlascaoid) was founded in 1987 and had P.J. Moriarty as the first chairman. It was a formidable group. An early decision was to seek a meeting with the Oireachtas Committee on the Gaeltacht. This took place in Leinster House.

A group of six, all Irish speakers, including the chairman, represented the Foundation. On the politicians' side were the Gaeltacht spokespersons from the various parties, including Michael D. Higgins, Dinny McGinley and Mary Coughlan. Again, all these were Irish speakers. The Chairman of the Oireachtas Committee was Senator Tom Fitzgerald from Dingle, a native Irish speaker and a good one at that.

With that kind of a line-up around the table in the committee room, it was expected that most of the contributions and discussions would be in Irish, although English was spoken at the committee for a variety of reasons.

Indeed I was very much the beneficiary of this approach on the one occasion I appeared at the committee. It was dealing with the media in general and, because of my own experience as a journalist on newspapers and television, I felt that I had some useful ideas to put forward. I was able to do this reasonably well in Irish, with the aid of prepared notes. However, when the discussion moved on, I really wasn't able to participate in any kind of a satisfactory manner. The chairman of the time, Dinny McGinley, regarded by many people in the country as one of the finest speakers of Irish heard on radio and television, came to my rescue and invited me, if I so wished, to speak in English. This was an offer I accepted and I hope I made a useful contribution.

Before the Blasket Island Foundation hearing commenced, the chairman, Senator Tom Fitzgerald, clarified the language position for everyone: 'Now lads, we're all very mature and grown-up here, so you can speak away in English if you wish.'

The Lost Isle

Charles J. Haughey, when Taoiseach, came into the Dáil Chamber for a scheduled vote just before the close of business. A pair would have been available to him if he so wished, but a Taoiseach, like every other Dáil deputy, likes to keep up a good average in Dáil votes.

In the short period the Taoiseach spent crossing the Chamber to his seat, he would have been able to pick up on something of the discussion then in progress. It was a motion for the adjournment in my name, a device sometimes used as a way of bringing local issues to the attention of the National Parliament.

The purpose of this motion was to get the support of the Dáil for local opposition to the plantation of a Sitka Spruce forest that would greatly curtail the vantage-points for viewing the Lake Isle of Innisfree and the general landscape still very much unchanged from the time that William Butler Yeats first visited there.

The Lake Isle in Lough Gill, or on Lough Gill as the locals say, has only one access road, over two miles long, 'twisty and windy'.

After the Dáil vote, many deputies waited on, as is the custom, until the Ceann Comhairle had announced the result. The Taoiseach was among them and when he spotted me he beckoned me to join him.

'What's all this about?' he asked. I explained, as I had just done in the Dáil, the undoubted difficulties that afforestation with Sitka Spruce would cause for the thousands of visitors who go out to Killery every summer to get a closer look at the Lake Isle, at Killery Point. The Taoiseach was quite obviously interested but said nothing definite or clear-cut before returning to his office. It was a good start.

I was never told and I never asked about any follow-up action that the Taoiseach might have taken, but now more than twenty years later there still has been no planting of a Sitka Spruce forest, the land is there much as it was then with an obviously contented flock of sheep keeping down the grass, and now, thankfully, planning permission is needed for any forestry work, as it should have been years earlier.

Without in any way diminishing the efforts of the Killery objectors, or indeed my own part in the campaign and that of my colleague, Deputy Mattie Brennan, who recited 'The Lake Isle of Innisfree' for the Dáil, word-perfect of course, I think that it is right to put on record that I believe the Taoiseach, Deputy Haughey, 'made enquiries'.

Back in Sligo they were delighted with the Taoiseach's interest. But the campaign against the Sitka Spruce afforestation had to be maintained. Where do you go after you believe you have won the support of the Taoiseach?

'You'll have to write a poem "after Yeats".' I tried that once before but it was a bit of a disaster, only saved by the fact that I was trying something different from the usual 'Dear Jim' letter to tell a supporter that the Minister for Justice was about to announce his appointment as a Peace Commissioner for the Barony of Leyney! He was to be made a PC but just to rhyme I called it the Fianna Fáil Political Degree.

They say that a politician will do anything for a vote and now I believe it. As far as publicity for the protest campaign, my verses 'after Yeats' were a big success, especially with the *Sunday Tribune* in two consecutive issues. Reaction from others was not so much negative as non-existent. My own Dáil colleagues, who have at the ready a package of words to meet any contingency, don't seem to have read any papers at all on the relevant days! My PC constituent got his revenge by sending me all his clinic work in rhyme for the next year.

The Lost Isle of Innisfree
(*after Yeats*)

> I will arise and go now, and go to Innisfree
> And a forest curtain build there, of leaf and tall trees made.
> Nine green rows will I have there, a wire for the wishing see,
> And whistle a tune in the tree-shroud glade.
>
> And I shall have a lease there, for lease brings yearly flow,
> Cash from the trees a-growing to where the cropper sings;
> There midnight's not a glimmer, and noon's without a glow,
> And evening's full of the Sitka's stings.
>
> I will arise and go now, for always night and day
> I feel the new sap rising in the timbers as they grow;

While I stand on the roadway, or on the pavements
  grey,
I feel it in the bank's cash flow.

A Priceless Heritage
— John Kelly

I heard Deputy Michael Noonan* talking about our
unique heritage and our unique cultural heritage and
our unique Irish language. I do not mean to point at
him in particular but he was the person who
mentioned it. In my years in the House, I rarely heard
him open his mouth in any language but never in
Irish. I do not know what his grip of the thing is or
how much interest he has in it. I am willing to
suppose he has not less than anybody else but that is
not a lot. What is a Dutchman to make of his
complaint that Irish has not been made one of the
Community's official languages? The Dutchman, if he
is the Dutchman I have met, will say: 'What is it in
your personal scale of priorities? Do you speak it
yourself? Say a few words for us in Irish that will not
just be the Our Father or the Apostles Creed that you
have learned off in school. Translate the conversation
we had about the abominable meal we had in the
railway station in Milan off the top of your head like
a good man until I hear what the thing sounds like.' I
do not believe that he, like a lot of other Members,
would be glad to be asked such a thing. Why then
does he expect the Dutchman or a Greek to take
seriously pleas of that kind? It would not have crossed
my mind to mention that, were it not for the fact that
I heard this bit of 1927-ish flim-flamery float across
the House from a man who must have heard it when

he was a small child from Dev who at least believed this stuff.

Dev at least believed what he was saying and went to some lengths to practise it, but they did not extend to forcing his followers to do so. He was willing to put up with the most perfunctory observance from them. As I said, he believed what he said and went to some lengths to practise it, and it rubbed off on the young Deputy Noonan. I can see him in his short trousers, with the wind whistling across the Square in Newcastle West, listening to Dev speaking from the back of a lorry and saying to himself that if he wanted to get on in politics, he would occasionally have to take off his cap to the Irish language and refer to its status as a unique cultural asset and inheritance.

That is the kind of talk no one outside these shores can understand because it does not come across as serious talk. The stranger judges us by what we do. What he sees when he comes to Ireland on holiday or on a business trip is the cultural situation. I mean 'cultural' in a general sense and not just the language we speak but the way we live, which, to his eyes, is barely distinguishable from what happens in England. There are the same boring rows of boring semi-detached houses, the same interests, the same sports, the same slang and jargon. We use expressions like 'no way' and 'hopefully', which nobody used 15 years ago, because the English do. He will see the same type of clothes, the same manners, the same places to go on holiday, the same standards of everything.

Where is this priceless heritage? I mean this only as an example of the awful isolation which our geographical situation forces on us. The sooner we get integrated in Europe and send streams and cycles of our young people to live there, the better.

Eventually some of them will come back, bringing with them skills and experience and, above all, a scale of values, a tariff of the importance of things, not necessarily taking over holus bolus from a German or a Greek, a tariff which will at least represent a modification of this peculiar Irish mentality in which sanctimonious hypocrisy, unreality, the willingness to know one thing but to believe, or pretend to believe, another are such significant parts. That form of mentality works detrimentally to us in industry, agriculture, industrial relations and politics.

The more we can integrate with people who will give us a standard to measure our own way of doing things, which will enable us to see when we are talking *seafóid* [nonsense], which will enable us to understand that we have been preaching something that is not a viable proposition, that will provide some standard by which we can measure our own beliefs, and perhaps modify them, the more we will benefit from it intellectually, and even spiritually, but certainly industrially, commercially, agriculturally and politically.

[Source: From one of John Kelly's speeches to the Dáil]

---

* There were two Michael Noonans in the Dáil at the time: Michael Noonan (Fianna Fáil), Limerick West, and Michael Noonan (Fine Gael), Limerick East. From the speech, it is obvious that the references were to Michael Noonan of Fianna Fáil, who served as a member and deputy for many years.

18. Notes from the Underbelly

The Political Ambush
— Nicholas Furlong

The art of destroying the platform speaker's confidence is an honourable one. That art is now denied to the plain people, but is maintained to a less glorious extent by the radio or TV presenter. Until the 1960s when television finally saw off the political rally at market squares, church gates and crossroads, political cunning demanded that opponents be reduced before the greatest number of people. It was my privilege in post-World War II years to note that art form at its most sinister.

The first political theatre I experienced was in Wexford's Bullring, drenched in the (innocent) blood of Cromwellian martyrs, a property brought frequently to mind. The protagonists were the Soldiers of the Rearguard, the Blue Shirts, the party of the working deprived and one volatile independent. It was the final rallies which provided the best prospect of torpedoing any candidate or cause below the waterline. For this, a special person was cultivated locally by each faction.

That special person had to be a male and a beer sponge, so that if roughly treated or the recipient of a clatter from a baton, few would fret. In all cases the disturbance-riser was from out of town, so not too well known except to the occupants of the smoke-filled party snug. The candidate and his platform acolytes must always exude gravitas and old-world courtesy while at the same time showing that they were no daws. A perceived connection with the bowsie was, however, to be made unthinkable.

Mr de Valera, whose very figure inspired awe, was the prime Blue Shirt target. Despite a tricolour and brass band escort from the town limits to the Bullring, Blue Shirts plan and ops. had their man already planted near the platform. He was a red-pussed dolt in a cap with the debris of a tomato sandwich smeared across his gob.

Mr de Valera, regarded by the Soldiers of the Rearguard as a saint, was not a Dillonesque orator, but he was solid and most impressive in a delivery which defied anything other than the incense of scriptural authority. However, the Blue Shirt was made of sterner stuff. Whenever An Taoiseach paused, your man from Ballymurn cocked his head aloft, cupped his hand to his mouth and shouted out in coached but mistaken pronunciation 'The Vampire! The human Vampire!' Incessantly it went until the inevitable incident.

Apoplexy claimed sensitive listeners but revenge was arranged in vicious style as the occasion warranted. General Richard Mulcahy was the principal speaker at the Fine Gael final rally. He was an excellent orator in both official languages. His

Wexford family connections were comprehensive. His wife was a member of the Tomcoole family of formidable academics, the Ryans. Typically the family had been terribly split in the Civil War, with another Ryan sister married to Seán T. O' Kelly while her brother, Dr Jim, was Dev's Minister for Agriculture and a Wexford TD.

The Fianna Fáil plant was a tall rustic, bald, with large eyes, a chewing jaw, amiable in his fearless ignorance. The whiff of Civil War cordite lingered so the dastardly plan was not merely to inspire trouble for General Mulcahy, but to toss havoc into the Blue Shirts and old Redmondite ranks at his back on the platform. So, in the usual pause, the planted Rearguard Soldier's gob opened and loudly hurled the question, 'How many did yez shoot?' Next time from the same tobacco-chewing mouth in stultifying relevance, 'What about the seventy-seven?'

These meetings had one common denominator. In all of them, untutored platform enemies, as distinct from plants, were down in the crowd to yell 'What did youze do?' Exclusive to the Labour ranks, at any farmer candidate was the screech, 'Dirty butter!' Such platform vulnerability was not shared by all candidates. Wexford constituency provided one exotic candidate, an independent who trusted no one, and whose tongue was feared by all. He was Mr Albert 'Bertie' Murphy, whose campaign manager, Mr Patrick 'Patsy' Furlong, had the high-pitched vocal range of a wasp.

Their platform policy, though unsuccessful, was determined to do away with rates, the land annuities, the Cromwellian confiscations and Mr de Valera. Mr Murphy and Mr Furlong were both hardship-bitten, well-read farmers who, through their nightly discussions on affairs of state, decided that anarchy obtained. They concluded that they would challenge it by soliciting the votes of fellow citizens in the 1937 and subsequent general elections.

Though devoid of adequate election capital, they won attention to their convictions by oratory which scorned etiquette or orthodoxy. The platform in Wexford's Bullring consisted of a hose-drawn dray. Mr Murphy's oratory attacked so many establishment positions that amongst them was a scripture-quoting neighbour of the Established Church. Mr Murphy responded to such quotes with instant logic, history and King James scriptural phrases he had invented himself.

However, since Mr de Valera was responsible for the 'aekenomic' war and the subsequent anarchy, Bertie Murphy launched a scornful deluge of derision at every speech, starting with the words 'and now the Spaniard. The Tay shook, if you like, and begob we are all rightly tay shook alright,' a reference to rationing (laughter and cheers, 'Good on ya, Bertie, oul stock', and so on). Mr Murphy continued, 'The man made his money running guns to Franco to put down the blacks.'

All political shades and circuit court barristers paid tribute to Bertie Murphy's speeches by attendance at his rallies. One was more obvious than others. He was a well-fleshed, large businessman of hot temper, a forthcoming Mayor of Wexford. The insult to the sacred person of his Chief caused him near apoplectic death. When he recovered, he shrieked at the candidate, 'That's a lie, you blasted blackguard.' Without drawing breath, Mr Murphy directed his election agent, Mr Furlong, with the words, 'Go over there at wanst, Patsy, and throw a sheaf of oats to the ass.'

The most devastating destruction of a candidate we must record took place at a final rally in Rathmines Town Hall, where the party of the high moral ground produced a gentleman of decency and unimpeachable propriety. He was the owner/manager of a ladies-wear emporium and had decades of selfless service in the Indigent Poor Society, the battered wives, schools' management, the Knights of Columbanus and the Dublin Chamber of Commerce. He was the appropriate man the canvassers promoted as the one 'who had a stake in the country'.

In his address he deplored the lapse in public morals, the absence of those whose integrity in public life saw them give their lives for their country and not for their pocket, 'men whom neither rank, reward or position could buy'. He drew comparison with the elected unclean of that day, when in developing his theme a terrible gravel voice resembling a bench saw was heard from platform to rear wall: 'Tell us about the mott you're living with down in the Monto.'

He carried on. Despite the speaker's bravery and beaded perspiration, the voice rumbled out at every advantageous break: 'Tell us about the mott you're living with down in the Monto.'

End of candidacy, and to paraphrase sacred scripture, the candidate 'was never more seen in those parts'.

[Nicholas Furlong: the Wexford writer and historian's recent works include *County Wexford in the Rare Oul' Times*, *Diarmait, King of Leinster* (Mercier) and *Young Farmer Seeks Wife*. He is a weekly feature writer in the Wexford Echo Group Newspapers.]

The Tip-off that Shattered a Cabinet

It was the most important tip-off in modern Irish politics. This wasn't the familiar newspaper leak. It went to the foundations and was handled in the main by Liam Cosgrave, Leader of the Opposition, and Jack Lynch, as Taoiseach. Stephen Collins in his book *The Cosgrave Legacy* follows the tip-off from its arrival on Garda notepaper until the government issued a statement that two Ministers, Charles J. Haughey and Neil Blaney, had been fired.

Stephen Collins

When the Dáil convened in early May 1970 the political system was plunged into a crisis which appeared at the time to threaten the foundations of the State. The arms crisis saw the Taoiseach, Jack Lynch, firing his two most powerful Ministers, one of them a future Taoiseach, and the resignation of two others because of a plot to import arms into the country.

Liam Cosgrave played a central role in the whole affair. He received two tip-offs about the plot a few days before the news burst on an unsuspecting public. One of the tip-offs came to him on Garda notepaper alleging that two Ministers, Charles Haughey and Neil Blaney, were involved.

Michael Mills, who was then political correspondent of the *Irish Press*, confirms the tip to Cosgrave and the names on the list. The tip-off is believed to have come from Chief Superintendent Phil McMahon, a retired head of the Special Branch, who because of his extensive knowledge and contacts had been retained by the Garda authorities as an advisor on subversion.

Cosgrave was stunned by the note and he showed it to a journalist and trusted friend, Ned Murphy, political correspondent of the *Sunday Independent*. Murphy made a copy and brought it to the editor of the *Sunday Independent*, Hector Legge. After some consideration, a decision was taken not to run with the story because of the difficulties of confirming the information and because Legge decided it would not be in the national interest.

When the Dáil next met on Tuesday 5 May, neither Jack Lynch nor the Ministers involved had any idea that Cosgrave was in possession of the crucial information. Lynch took TDs by surprise by announcing to the Chamber at the beginning of the day's business that Micheál Ó Móráin, the Minister for Justice, who had no connection with the plot, had resigned. Cosgrave was on his feet immediately to ask: 'Can the Taoiseach say if this is the only Ministerial resignation we can expect?'

'I do not know what the deputy is referring to,' replied Lynch, to which Cosgrave responded: 'Is it only the tip of the iceberg?'

Cosgrave went on to make the cryptic comment that the Taoiseach could deal with the situation and he added that smiles were very noticeable by their absence on the Government benches. Most TDs and journalists had no idea what Cosgrave was talking about and Lynch still didn't get the message that Cosgrave knew what was going on. When nothing further had happened by that night Cosgrave wasn't sure what was happening and he began to wonder whether the tip-offs he had received were designed to trap.

He decided to consult a few of his closest colleagues that evening and ask their advice. Those present were Tom O'Higgins, Michael O'Higgins, Mark Clinton, Denis Jones and Jim Dooge.

Cosgrave told his colleagues there was something

he wanted to tell them. He said he had received a tip-off about a plot to import arms.

'I want your advice. What should I do? Is this a plant? Is someone trying to plant this on me to make me go over the top?' he asked his colleagues.

'We argued first of all as to whether he could take it as being something he could act on, because he feared the danger of just being hoist on [sic] a petard. And we came to the conclusion that yeh, on balance, we had to act.' Having agreed on this Cosgrave said he had a second question about the form of action he should take. 'What do I do? Do I bring it up in the Dáil? Do I go to the newspapers? Do I go to the Taoiseach?' he asked.

Mark Clinton was the first one who spoke and he said: 'I think this is of such national importance the only thing is to go to the Taoiseach and go to him tonight.' The others present agreed.

'And Liam went off and rang Jack Lynch's office and established that Jack was still in Leinster House. The Dáil had risen and Liam went off for a while and we all sat around wondering what was happening, and he came back and I always remember it, he sort of stood in the door and closed the door behind him and then he looked up and looked at us and said, "It's all true." I will always remember that. And then he called a front-bench meeting for the following morning,' said one of the people present that night.

Following Cosgrave's visit Lynch spoke personally to Blaney and phoned Haughey. He asked both men to resign but they refused. He then went home to consult his wife, Máirín, and at 2 am he instructed the head of the Government Information Service, Eoin Neeson, to issue a statement that Haughey and Blaney had been fired.

Lynch took action that night as a direct response to Cosgrave's intervention. The Peter Berry diaries, published in *Magill* in 1980, show that the Taoiseach had decided a week earlier to bury the whole incident and even during the Dáil exchanges on 5 May Lynch does not appear to have grasped that Cosgrave knew of the whole affair. It was only when the Fine Gael leader went to him that night that he was catapulted into action.

Fine Gael's Peter Barry recalls speaking in the Dáil that evening on a financial resolution.

'It was about 6.30 or 7 pm on a Tuesday evening, the only time a backbencher can get a slot. I was less than a year in the Dáil and it was one of my early speeches. The next morning the Taoiseach, Jack Lynch, comes in, pushes Johnny Geoghegan aside and starts interrupting me. "How do you justify that? Where did you get that figure?" So it wasn't on his mind at 7 o'clock that he had any problems.'

The Dáil record for that evening bears out Peter Barry's memory; he was heckled three times by the Taoiseach during his speech shortly before 7 pm.

When the Dáil met at 11.30 am on 6 May the sensational news of the dismissal of the two Ministers, Haughey and Blaney, had convulsed the country. A third, Kevin Boland, resigned in protest, along with parliamentary secretary Paudge Brennan. Lynch proposed to a stunned Dáil that the day's sitting be postponed until 10 pm that night to give his parliamentary party an opportunity to discuss the issue. Cosgrave reluctantly agreed while making the point that a Fianna Fáil party meeting should not take precedence over the business of the country.

When the Dáil met at 10 pm on the night of 6 May the motion before the house was simply for the appointment of Des O'Malley as Minister for Justice in place of Micheál Ó Mórain but Lynch made it clear he was prepared to debate all the issues involved in the arms crisis ... he had asked Haughey and Blaney to resign a week earlier....They had asked for time to consider their positions and he agreed but had again asked for their resignations the previous evening. When they refused he had terminated their appointments.

'I may say that on the question of suspicion Deputy Cosgrave came to me yesterday evening to say he had some information from an anonymous source connecting the two Ministers with this alleged attempt at unlawful importation.'

Cosgrave then rose to speak.

'Last night at approximately 8 pm I considered it my duty in the national interest to inform the Taoiseach of information I had received and which indicates a situation of such gravity for the nation that it is without parallel in the country since the foundation of the State. By approximately 10 pm two Ministers had been dismissed and a third had resigned.... Yesterday when I received a copy of a document on official garda notepaper which supported the information already at my disposal and which also included some additional names, I decided to put the facts in my possession before the Taoiseach.'

[Stephen Collins, *The Cosgrave Legacy*, Blackwater Press, 1996]

19. A Final Bow

Streets

Although I retired from active politics ten years ago, it is still hard to resist doing the old TD routine, when someone stops me for a chat in Sligo town or some other part of the constituency of Sligo–Leitrim. From talks with colleagues in the Irish Parliamentary (Former Members) Association, I know that they found it equally difficult to shake the habits acquired on the voting trail.

The start with me was always a lengthy handshake. Not always because I was particularly pleased to see the person, but just as often I was stretching the time in the hope that the constituent's name might come to me. Names were usually my problem.

On this occasion there was no trouble at all with the surname, Leheny, or the townland in south Sligo where he lived. I just couldn't remember the first name and was a bit surprised to find myself candidly admitting as much. That kind of admission I would never even consider if I were still a serving Dáil deputy. You pretend that you know everyone and then be prepared with an exit plan of some dignity from the conversation, just in case.

The name here turned out to be Anthony; his politics I did not know. Because of his age bracket, I could assume they were the same now as they had been in my time in Leinster House. Whatever might happen in other parts of the country, you don't get rapid political swings in south Sligo, certainly since the Owenmore river drainage was removed from the agenda. The feeling I had, however, was that Anthony Leheny was not 'one of ours'. I could remember calling at his house on a canvass at several general elections, speaking to him at length on the doorstep and never ending up with more than a 'good luck anyway'.

I believe that that particular response of 'good luck anyway' is about the most negative message any candidate can get and is delivered solely in the interests of courtesy. Translated into political terms, I believe it means 'You're all right. We have nothing against you. But there are no votes here for you.' Because of this feeling about Anthony's political allegiance, I decided that it might be as well to steer clear of that subject. We had met on the new complex of roads and streets that has transformed traffic on the western side of Sligo town and, as a bonus, provided spectacular views of Benbulben as you drive by. For a bit of fun, however, I asked Anthony if he was aware that we were walking down the newly christened Ted Nealon Drive.

'Arrah ... which Nealon would that be?' was the response.

'I suppose myself, so *The Sligo Champion* said anyway.'

'Huh ... I thought that you had to be dead before they did that kind of a thing — called a street after you.... Well, good luck anyway,' were Anthony's farewell words as he headed off in the direction of McSharry Road.

My Confirmation Day
— Feargal Nealon

There are no pictures of my confirmation day on the walls of our home. I never got my photograph taken with the bishop. I didn't even get the coke and Rice Krispies cakes in the social centre afterwards. There was apparently a search party out for me in the surrounds of Carraroe church, until my mother realised that my Granny Loughnane and Uncle Brendan were missing as well.

Brendan loved his Guinness and he enjoyed the banter about sport and politics over a few pints. To that end, myself and my only sister Louise were escorted into his car as soon as the Mass had ended, and along with our granny headed for the restaurant where the family had organised a meal for ten or so guests.

The particular restaurant was a good half hour's drive from Carraroe church, deep into rural south Sligo. As we followed the signs off the main road, we came across a quaint old country pub — the type of place where Brendan knew the Guinness would have to be good. The pub was empty except for the owner and one farmer who was drinking at the counter. We sat down by the fireplace. Brendan winked at myself and Louise and let on that we were his kids. He then went on to play the role of a wealthy tycoon down from Dublin, thus explaining how we were so well dressed.

After some talk with the lads and another wink in our direction, he enquired, 'This is Ted Nealon country, I believe?'

The owner immediately piped up, 'That auld bollox, he was supposed to come to a meeting here a few months back … never showed up. Don't talk to me about that man.' Brendan swiftly changed the subject for the sake of our young ears and talked GAA for a while. Just as he was coming toward the end of his pint, the pub door opens and in comes Dad.

'Well, so this is where ye got to!'

The Admirer

I was with a group of colleagues in a corner of the Members' Bar in Leinster House when a call came through for Deputy Paul McGrath, who was with us. A friend was in Doheny & Nesbitt's pub in nearby Lower Baggot Street. Would Paul join him there?

'Why don't we all join him there?' came the suggestion from someone else. 'A change of scenery will do us no harm.' So we walked out Leinster Lawn, down Merrion Street to Doheny & Nesbitt's, where it was standing room only. A lot of the patrons in this pub prefer to talk than to rest or to do almost anything else.

When the Members' Bar group finally assembled, there was Paul McGrath (and his friend), Dinny McGinley, Michael Ring, Pádraic McCormack and myself.

After a few minutes Michael Ring tugged me by my coat and whispered: 'In the party standing near us there is a very well-dressed lady and she definitely knows one of us; she knows you or she knows me, and I think it's me. Don't look now, but do when you get a chance. I don't want to be embarrassed if she comes over here, and she turns out to be a constituent I don't know.' I did as Michael suggested but, to me, the lady was a stranger.

Sure enough, however, after a short while she did come across towards our group and, greatly to my glee, passed by Deputy Ring and approached me!

'You're Ted Nealon, you used to be on television,' she said. I had an idea of what was coming up next. The first thing was to make sure my colleagues were listening and would hear any compliments. So I introduced each of them individually to her, with, in cases, some substantial additions to the contributions they were making as legislators. There followed the usual banter of occasions like this, and then it was time for our new friend to get back to her own group.

'I'm delighted now I came over to speak to you, Ted. I'm going home to Tipperary for the weekend and I'll be able to tell them that I met you. My mother was a great admirer of yours on television.'

The laughter of Michael Ring surely could be heard at the butt of Croagh Patrick! And my other good friends were not too far behind.

Before the night was out, Deputy Ring had retold the story a number of times, adding colourful embellishments along the way. As we came to closing time, he was on his latest. This time it was not the Tipperary lady's mother who was a great admirer of mine, it was her grandmother!

Sometimes it's safer to stick with the quiet of the Members' Bar!

Index